# 積ん読
# TSUNDOKU

# The Japanese Art of Collecting Books

# TSUNDOKU

積ん読

TAIKI
RAITO
PYM

C CASSELL

First published in Great Britain in 2026 by Cassell, an imprint of
Octopus Publishing Group Ltd
Carmelite House, 50 Victoria Embankment
London EC4Y 0DZ
www.octopusbooks.co.uk

An Hachette UK Company
www.hachette.co.uk

The authorized representative in the EEA is Hachette Ireland,
8 Castlecourt Centre, Dublin 15, D15 XTP3, Ireland (email: info@hbgi.ie)

Original title: *Tsundoku: L'arte giapponese di accumulare libri*
Original project: Studio Pym/Milan
Concept: Lucia Stipari, Gianluca Bavagnoli
Italian texts: Alice Scieghi
Illustrator: Chiara Collinassi

Copyright © 2025 Giunti Editore S.p.A., Firenze-Milano
www.giunti.it
Translation copyright © 2026 Octopus Publishing Group

All rights reserved. No part of this work may be reproduced
or utilized in any form or by any means, electronic or mechanical,
including photocopying, recording or by any information storage and
retrieval system, without the prior written permission of the publisher.

ISBN: 9781788406468
eISBN: 9781788406475

A CIP catalogue record for this book is available from the British Library.

Printed and bound in Great Britain.
10 9 8 7 6 5 4 3 2 1

English Translation: Raph Torrance in association with
First Edition Translations Ltd, Cambridge, UK.

Publisher: Trevor Davies
Senior Managing Editor: Sybella Stephens
Creative Director: Jonathan Christie
Production Controller: Sarah Parry

This FSC® label means that materials used for the product have been responsibly sourced.

*To the people who, just like stories,
have the power to make us feel at home.*

# CONTENTS

*Introduction*
More Books than You Could Ever Hope to Read 1

1. **The Books Around Us Contain Mysteries** 19
2. **Buying a Book** 31
3. **A House Full of Books** 71
4. **Books Left Unread** 91
5. **When Reading Feels Like Climbing a Mountain** 117
6. **Books with a Little 'B'** 145
7. **The Other Side of the Coin** 157

*Conclusion*
The Books of Your *Kokoro* ♥ 169
Any Excuse to Hoard More Books! 175
*Tsundoku* Diary of Unread Books 183

Introduction
# MORE BOOKS THAN YOU COULD EVER HOPE TO READ

Izumi wakes up early every day, and today is no exception. She enjoys gazing out of the window, watching the sun's rays turn ever-warmer shades of yellow as she lingers over her breakfast.

She leaves the house and begins walking – quickly, yet never rushing – without having to think about where she's going. She lets her feet lead the way: after all, by now they know it by heart. She enters her local bookshop, her favourite, then leaves again a little while later. Her feet automatically take her back home, one in front of the other – walking slowly, yet never dawdling.

Tucked into her tote bag, she has a book on the language of flowers, its pages full of drawings printed on the thick paper reserved for beautiful books. The sky is quickly clouding over, and the wind has picked up. A sudden gust blows her hair over her eyes. She tries to smooth it back into place with one arm, but doesn't quite manage to, as her hands are full with a mystery novel – the latest outing of her favourite detective – and a book with a cover that offers no clue as to what lies within. She had taken them out of her bag to flick through as she wandered home.

The moment she gets home, she sets the books down on the table, sinks into the sofa and closes her eyes. A ray of sunshine peeks through the clouds, warming her legs. She opens her eyes again.

In an attempt to make a little room and get comfy on the sofa, she moves a couple of books onto the coffee table in front of her, placing one on top of the pile in the middle and the other on the one next to it: the central pile has grown a smidge too tall and now seems dangerously rickety. The overflowing bookcase opposite her is an explosion of colours. Although it was once neat and tidy, her orderly arrangement has been undermined, disrupted by the new books she has tried to squeeze into every last nook and cranny, adding a horizontal row in front of the others, wedging in any oversized books diagonally . . .

Izumi gets up and readjusts one that she worries is about to come tumbling down. She runs her fingertips along the entire bookcase, then turns the corner that separates it from the hallway, where she immediately comes across another. This one is where some of the denser volumes can be found: the hallway bookcase is home to all the reference books, which is a delight to cast your eyes over as you walk past; it is positively brimming with interesting things you can learn about a little at a time. It is seven steps wide from edge to edge.

The bedroom door, open just a sliver, offers a glimpse of her double futon, which is wedged between shelves crammed with romance and mystery novels: the perfect diversion for when you wake up at the crack of dawn and can't get back to sleep.

Before going to the bathroom, Izumi goes back into the lounge, picks up her latest acquisition – the new mystery novel – and delicately balances it on top of one of the piles on her bedside table. Nobody glancing at the tabletop would be able to discern whether it was made from light wood or dark, but it really doesn't matter.

# MORE BOOKS THAN YOU COULD EVER HOPE TO READ

Finally, Izumi heads into the bathroom for a steaming hot shower. She slides the glass door open, gently moves the stool out of the way – being careful not to tip over the stack of books sitting on it – then takes a big, fluffy towel out of the cupboard and hangs it on the hook on the wall. Then she turns on the water.

If you found yourself smiling and nodding as you read this, your nostrils filling with the heady, wholly irresistible scent of crisp new pages, then it can mean only one thing. Your love of books is boundless, buying them is a source of immense joy, and . . . well, you live in a home with something rather peculiar about it: bedside tables buried under teetering piles of books, bookcases vast enough to accommodate second and even third rows, cupboards hiding the shame of duplicates purchased by mistake, shelves that threaten to crash to the ground at any moment under the weight of countless colourful recipe books, sofas surrounded by makeshift walls of beautifully bound classics, orderly columns of timeless British literature lining the hallways . . . and a passion, an urge, that could see every last gap in the house being stuffed with books before long.

All these books seem to be sitting there, patiently waiting. But waiting for what? For the right moment, of course: the moment when you finally crack them open and set about reading them. A moment – it is worth bearing in mind – that might never even come.

Because of the ten books you buy today, you might read one or two within the next year, with three or four more earmarked for holidays or 'when you've finally got some free time', but you can be sure that the rest will stay there perfectly untouched, peering down at you, cluttering up every home you have over the years, following you each time you move house.

積ん読 – TSUNDOKU

## LIVING ON BOOKS ALONE

Let's try to calculate statistically – at a rough approximation – the maximum number of books that one person could theoretically get through in their lifetime, assuming that this hypothetical person decides to dedicate their entire existence to reading. There are, on average, 300 pages in a book, each of which contains 300 words. The average reading speed is 200 words per minute. If we assume these figures to be true, then it follows that we can read a standard book (90,000 words) in 7½ hours. Now, if we set aside 8 hours for sleeping and another hour for dealing with our basic needs, let us assume that we can spend all our remaining time reading: 15 hours a day. If the average lifespan is around 80 years, and we assume that this person started reading at the age of 5, then they could get through a dizzying 54,788 books in their lifetime.

Seems like an absurd number, right?

But in 2010, Google conducted some research that will blow your mind. The question was: how many books are there in the world? The result was staggering: in 2010, there were no fewer than 129,864,880 unique books in the world.

Given that more than two million new books are released every year, by the time this book hits the shelves of your local shop, that number will be somewhere closer to 160 million.

Which means that, even with a life dedicated exclusively to reading, there would still be a mammoth 159,945,212 books you would have to miss out on.

So although this is just napkin maths, with some rather extreme assumptions, it nonetheless gives us a clear idea of the pitifully small number of books we are capable of reading over the course of our entire existence – a drop in the ocean compared to the millions on the market!

# MORE BOOKS THAN YOU COULD EVER HOPE TO READ

Don't you feel sad at the thought of the many pages whose content is destined to remain unknown to you, adventures that will never transport you to the far-off realms of your dreams, fantastical lands that you will never explore?

Not exactly, right?

It would be more accurate to say that, when struck by the sight of all the books that you own but will never manage to read, the feeling that washes over your body is more like a mix of melancholy and euphoria, a unique emotion that nothing else is quite capable of stirring up.

So... doesn't that at least discourage you from buying any more books?

Not in the slightest!

> There is nothing like dreaming about walking into a bookshop, sifting through the second-hand tables or surrendering to the delights of the infinite options at a book fair just so that enthusiasm once again floods your heart and that gentle, tingling itch on your fingertips grows into a frenzy.

Worried you might be a weirdo?

Absolutely not, don't you fret: you're in good company here. There's even a name especially for people like you, a single word that contains an action but also conjures up that bittersweet feeling that we have come to revel in over the years. It is no coincidence that the term is taken from Japanese, which is the language of symbols par excellence.

積ん読 – TSUNDOKU

## SO WHAT IS *TSUNDOKU*?

*Tsundoku* (積ん読) describes the act of procuring reading material, then allowing it to accumulate around your house without ever reading it or, in many cases, even flicking through it. It is also used to refer to the books left on a shelf or bedside table, just waiting for that perfect moment to come around: the (in)famous 'pile of shame'.

The word *tsundoku* brings together two elements: *tsunde-oku* (積んでおく, stockpiling things to make sure they're ready to use later, then forgetting about them for a while) and *dokusho* (読書, reading books). It doesn't means forgetting them forever – or at least, that's not the intention of whoever bought those books – but certainly for a good long while.

The term *tsundoku* originated in the Meiji Era (1868–1912) as a dialect word.

The Meiji Era was a busy time for Japan: it was a period of vast, sweeping changes, destined to alter the course of the country's history and future forever, so much so that it is also referred to as the 'Meiji Restoration'.

Up to that point, the Land of the Rising Sun had been stuck in the past and completely closed off from the outside world, both economically and socially. The Japanese had been used to their insular perspective, always looking inwards, and so they became a world of their own – a world within the world. Although this had serious repercussions in terms of stifling development and innovation, it did allow Japan to foster a culture with a marked identity, deeply rooted in its age-old traditions.

Change came swiftly and unexpectedly: in the space of a mere 50 years (from 1850 to the early 1900s), waves of profound upheaval swept the country.

The Japanese felt the earth crumbling beneath their feet, shaken by change so rapid that it threatened to undermine the

MORE BOOKS THAN YOU COULD EVER HOPE TO READ

very foundations of the precious culture they had so assiduously nurtured. Why? Because this dramatic change did not sprout spontaneously from within the island nation, where the inhabitants were used to watching everything unfold before their eyes. In July 1853, US Commodore Matthew Perry led four warships to the port of Uraga, near what is now known as Tokyo Bay, on the principal Japanese island of Honshu. The point of the warships descending upon the island was clearly to intimidate the locals, with Perry's ultimatum sending a chilling message: if the Japanese did not agree to end their isolation and open up to foreign trade, their shores would be bombed to smithereens.

And so, in the interests of avoiding a devastating conflict, the shogun – who had political control of the country – was forced to accept and sign agreements that would see Japan finally engaging in trade with other nations.

### A NEW STATUS QUO

Japan opening up resulted in a variety of outcomes: while the country underwent an impressive flurry of modernization, the sudden switch from a rural to an industrial economy and the upsetting of the existing social structure were violent enough to rend Japan in two. The price to pay for modernization was a deep divide in the country.

However, when the hostilities were finally over, Japan wholeheartedly embraced the new status quo. As in many similar situations, the image of flowers blooming out of the rubble or ashes of destruction fits like a glove. The crack that had been opened up by the world on the other side of the ocean found the strength to heal itself in nothing less than Japan's newfound drive towards the innovative, the other, the unknown. Opening the Japanese economy up to foreign trade made the country what it is today, and engaging with different cultures and societies allowed the rigid caste system to evolve and modernize.

Democracy was knocking at the door, bringing with it a whole new climate. The capital was moved from Kyoto to Edo, which was later renamed Tokyo. Once the modern world hit Japan's shores, it advanced across the island nation in leaps and bounds: the telegraph, the postal system, the yen, fashionable clothing from the West ... the lives of everyone in the Land of the Rising Sun changed radically overnight. Their tried-and-tested ways of communicating, getting around and paying – but also dressing and behaving – were suddenly transformed and would never be the same again. The educational system was reformed and the country was reorganized.

> Just as every last aspect of life was changing before the very eyes of the Japanese, they coined the term *tsundoku*, to refer to those who filled their homes with books without reading them, purely for the pleasure of owning them.

It was as if their attachment to books and what they represent – a link to the past and to tradition, knowledge as a form of love for the habits and customs of yesteryear, the rapidly fading ways of life – could offer a kind of anchor capable of steadying a ship tossed about by a stormy sea.

In a way – and this is still true today, if you think about it – books have always been a soothing source of comfort and security. They are tangible, material relics of a time long before us that will continue to endure long after we are gone. Something that occupies a space in the world, never changing as the years roll by and humankind's many conflicts rage on. And whether we devour their pages over and over again or never so much as glance at the wisdom within, their words will never change.

There is something reassuring about the thought of books as eternal elements that fill our homes, sturdy and weighty enough that the wind will never be able to blow them away.

## BIBLIOMANIA, BIBLIOPHILIA AND *TSUNDOKU*

It is fascinating to consider that the word *tsundoku* never made it out of Japan after it was coined. In European languages, there is a word to denote a love of books (*bibliophilia*) and another for an obsession with books (*bibliomania*), but somehow, this third nuance has not made its way into our lexicon. Bibliophilia, bibliomania and *tsundoku* are similar, yet nonetheless distinct concepts. They all have something to do with books, reading, love and a splash of obsession, but these factors are combined in different ways.

*Bibliophilia* – from the Greek βιβλίον (meaning 'book') and Φιλία (meaning 'love') – is a love of books.

A *bibliophile* is someone who harbours a deep passion for everything relating to books. What's more, they are usually seasoned connoisseurs of all the different editions, especially the rarest, most precious and valuable ones. The bibliophile spends a great deal of their time frequenting libraries and archives. An understatement, perhaps: indeed, it is thanks to bibliophiles that libraries and archives came about in the first place. We owe their very existence to these people, who appreciated the value of books and sought out a way to preserve their beauty. Bibliophiles are ardent believers in spreading culture, in the power of the knowledge that is shared when we read good writing.

Thanks to their ability to recognize a high-quality edition, bibliophiles are worshippers of the book as an object, but also capable of grasping its cultural and political value above and beyond its aesthetic and economic worth.

Bibliophiles are avid readers, though in many countries you only need to read 12 books a year to earn the title.

For the bibliophile, owning the books they love is a secondary consideration: reading or simply admiring them provides enough enjoyment. They have a vast library of their own, of course, but also love to linger around public spaces that can be a magnet for books and readers.

## A Bibliophile's Home

If you imagine the home of a bibliophile, it might conjure up the image of a neat, orderly bookcase containing shelves enclosed by glass doors, protecting their precious historical editions from dust. But at the same time, those doors are never sealed under lock and key: bibliophiles love to show off their treasures to other people – not to brag about them, but as a way of sharing their love and knowledge. They fully expect other people to treat books with the same care and reverence, considering their value to be universally obvious.

Indeed, in a bibliophile's home, you would never find books strewn carelessly about, used as knick-knacks on mantelpieces, tossed on the floor or with dogeared pages used as makeshift bookmarks.

*Bibliomania*, on the other hand – from the Greek βιβλίον (meaning 'book') and μανία (meaning 'mania') – is an obsession with books.

It is an obsessive-compulsive disorder that presents as a form of disposophobia, or hoarding disorder. As such, it is first and foremost a pathology, and therefore affects the sufferer's quality of life.

A bibliomaniac does not follow any conscious will to choose, as they cannot suppress their impulse to buy and accumulate books, at the considerable expense of their personal and social wellbeing. Their disorder often dominates their relationships: the unshakeable urge to acquire more and more books always takes precedence, leaving no room for compromise or anything (or, indeed, anyone) else.

The bibliomaniac often becomes attached to unique and valuable editions, or obsesses over owning every existing edition of a particular title. Those who suffer from this debilitating condition can even devote their entire lives to searching for a specific tome, bound in a particular year at a particular bindery and bearing the author's signature.

And yet, paradoxically, a bibliomaniac is not necessarily an avid reader. For someone like this, accumulating books has nothing to do with reading them. A bibliomaniac buys books for the sole purpose of owning them and increasing the size of their collection.

> In a way, bibliomania can be considered a degeneration of bibliophilia, wherein love becomes obsession and, as such, loses sight of everything that made it love in the first place.

For bibliomaniacs, the love of books is wholly replaced by the anxiety triggered by not owning a particular volume.

### A Bibliomaniac's Home

If you imagine their home, you will see a space entirely overrun with books. Books on the floor, books on the beds, books on top of cupboards, books everywhere you look. Every possible edition of a book with the same title – hundreds of copies which, to the untrained eye, may seem identical.

The bibliomaniac's house has been taken over by books and rendered uninhabitable. Sacrificed at this altar is the living space of whoever lives there, often along with their health and hygiene.

積ん読 – TSUNDOKU

## A *TSUNDOKU*-ER'S VIEW OF BOOKS AND READING

In light of this, *tsundoku* can be seen as a meeting point of sorts between bibliophilia and bibliomania. Those who fall into this third category buy books fully intending to read them, just ... at some point in the future.

They find the presence of books in their home reassuring, and certainly not a source of anxiety, as is often the case with bibliomaniacs.

Much like bibliophiles, those who tend towards *tsundoku* are avid readers and find reading to be a positive stimulus for their wellbeing. They feel no hint of distress at seeing the unread books at the top of their pile gradually being buried under new ones on a daily basis, because they are firm in their belief that, sooner or later, they will get around to reading every single book they have bought.

Though countless volumes may occupy every corner of the house – never graced with the same orderly cataloguing considered so crucial by bibliophiles – they never impinge upon the living space of its residents: on the contrary, they often serve as an original furnishing in their own right.

> The tsundoku category often includes omnivorous readers who, rather than accumulating particularly rare or valuable editions, stockpile books that they intend to read as they consider them interesting and unmissable.

MORE BOOKS THAN YOU COULD EVER HOPE TO READ

### A *Tsundoku*-er's Home

While the homes of bibliomaniacs and bibliophiles – who often organize their bookcases according to criteria of objective value, shared by the community of collectors of rare editions – tell us precious little about who they truly are, as we shall see, we need only cast the briefest of glances over the titles and covers of the books filling the homes of *tsundoku* practitioners to open up a clear window into their soul.

# How deep is your love of books?

1. When you open the first cupboard you see as you walk through your front door . . .
   a. There is a handful of books.
   b. There are only books and nothing else.
   c. There are no books.

2. Find the book you have the most duplicates of at home. How many copies are there?
   a. Four.
   b. Two or three.
   c. I don't own any duplicates!

3. How many books do you have on your bedside table?
   a. The one I'm reading, plus a few extra to leaf through every now and then.
   b. If only I could see my bedside table . . .
   c. Just the one I'm reading.

4. You decide to have some friends over for dinner . . .
   a. I can't wait to show them all the new books I bought!
   b. Hang on, I have to get all the books off the table . . .
   c. Looking forward to a lovely, relaxing evening.

5. Where is your happy place?
   a. The library.
   b. Home.
   c. A quiet outdoor spot where I can read in peace.

MORE BOOKS THAN YOU COULD EVER HOPE TO READ

6. When you're packing your suitcase for a trip, what do you do with your books?
    a. I never pack them in my suitcase because I'm afraid they'll be damaged.
    b. I only bring the one I'm currently reading, leaving a little space in my suitcase for a few new purchases.
    c. I bring the one I'm reading plus a few more, just in case.

## Answers

*You answered mostly (a):*
You're a bibliophile. Your love for books knows no limits and you adore sharing it with others.

*You answered mostly (b):*
You fall into the category of those who 'live *tsundoku*'. You love buying books, even though you know that you won't read them right away (and perhaps never will). This book is all about you!

*You answered mostly (c):*
You are, quite simply, a great lover of books. You see books as treasures because of the boundless stories they contain. You can't wait to immerse yourself in new worlds and go on new adventures.

# What kind of reader are you?

1. What's the first thing you do when you get home with a new book?
   a. Record a new video for TikTok.
   b. Leaf through it.
   c. Look for somewhere to put it.

2. How do you choose the books you buy?
   a. I follow the recommendations I find on social media.
   b. I judge it by its cover.
   c. I consider whether I'm interested in the topic.

3. How often do you find yourself buying an aesthetically ugly book?
   a. Never.
   b. Rarely.
   c. Often.

4. When you walk into a bookshop, where do you head first?
   a. To the BookToker section.
   b. To the new arrivals.
   c. To the fiction or classics section.

5. Your books are:
   a. Full of Post-It notes.
   b. Immaculate.
   c. Depends on how many times I've read them!

6. How are your bookcases arranged?
   a. By colour.
   b. By genre.
   c. In alphabetical order or by publisher.

# MORE BOOKS THAN YOU COULD EVER HOPE TO READ

## Answers

*You answered mostly (a):*
You're a social reader. Your home is filled with all the latest, trendiest books. You love sharing your life with other people, and your book preferences are a big part of that.

*You answered mostly (b):*
You're an omnivorous reader. Your priority is to have books with you at all times, no matter which ones: you love them all! Asking you to choose would be like asking a parent which child they love best.

*You answered mostly (c):*
You're a critical reader. You love your books because of the captivating stories they tell, the intriguing topics they delve into. You don't care what the cover looks like – you're only interested in the content.

# 1
# THE BOOKS AROUND US CONTAIN MYSTERIES

When Izumi started accumulating more books than she could ever hope to read, she almost didn't even notice. She didn't notice that her bookcase was gradually filling up and that the shelves that had seemed so sad and bereft when she first moved into her new place now had fewer and fewer empty spots. And when, one morning, she realized that the books she had just bought would no longer fit, she simply started a second row, then a third horizontal one, to squeeze them into the last remaining corners. When that space also finally ran out, she started arranging them on her bedside table. 'I'll just put the ones I'm going to read next on here,' she said to herself. And so she continued. First the bedroom, then the lounge, the kitchen – even the bathroom!

Then, suddenly one afternoon, she stopped and looked around. It hit her in a flash. The scales fell from her eyes in an instant and she finally saw her home for how it was. So she set about trying to fix the situation. She started sorting everything out, shifting piles of books here and there, dreaming up alternative solutions, carving out entirely new spaces. She went on lifting, moving, cleaning and tidying. All the while, the vibrant glow of Tokyo by night streamed in through her window, the colourful radiance of the signs never wavering for an instant.

The neon lights kept her company, growing brighter – whitish, almost – until Izumi finally realized that morning had broken. At this point she placed the book she had in her hand on the floor and, without touching another thing, crawled into her futon. Sleep washed over her as the light became warmer and brighter, illuminating the wooden floor, the overflowing bookcase, the piles that had been relocated to their new homes: in other words, the books that were still all over the place.

Deep down, people who live by the principle of *tsundoku* know full well that they will never manage to wade through all the books they own, the oceans of paper filling their homes. And one might be tempted to imagine that this sometimes sparks anxiety, discouragement, or even – at some point – a refusal to go on buying new books, at least for a little while.

But that's not the case for these eccentric individuals. Whenever they stop to dwell upon their overcrowded bookcases, the piles of books surrounding them, the new arrivals that have buried their bedside table and every last uncluttered surface, they are struck by what can only be described as a sort of revelation.

Imagine the scene. Their gaze meanders over all those volumes, drawn to the graphic elements that envelop them, making them unique; their attention is caught by:

# THE BOOKS AROUND US CONTAIN MYSTERIES

* Titles and subtitles.
* The blurb inscribed on the back cover.
* The dust jackets bearing praise from other writers, or a particularly significant quotation.

Then, as their fingers gently begin to leaf through the pages ... there it is: the realization that, even with the best will in the world, they will never have the time or opportunity to go any further, to absorb all the words contained between those spellbinding covers. It would take lifetimes upon lifetimes.

> It is as if books, by their very presence, make the idea of passing time tangible and yet, at the same time, reassure us that we play an active part in those passing hours, days and years.

The bitter realization that nothing can be done to stop time from storming by swiftly and inexorably, as well as the sense of resignation we feel when faced with all the volumes that will remain on those shelves untouched, disappear in a puff of smoke, torn through by the vital force that every object with great potential – and a book very much falls into this category – contains within itself.

It is a vital force that prompts us to look to the future through the enthusiastic eyes of someone who sees an infinite sprawl of time before them. This sensation is not discouraging. Far from it: it is inebriating.

The mere realization of how much, in theory, there is to read, to know, to imagine, immediately puts us face to face with the concept of infinity, forces us to appreciate the sheer beauty of the world and all the wondrous possibilities it has to offer; pausing to drink in the vastness of everything around us makes us feel tiny and powerless, but at the same time viscerally alive and euphoric at the idea of being part of something so much bigger than ourselves.

After all, contemplating the books we have acquired over the years is not a far cry from what happens when we gaze up at the night sky. Observing the stars translates into admiring something so very vast and far away that it manages to make us feel at once infinitely small and, strangely, at total peace, occupying our place in the universe.

It is by no means a distressing realization. Instead, it conjures up a sort of bittersweet sadness, brimming with hope.

> Those who surround themselves with books experience the same feelings of vastness and immense potential as when they wander out to gaze up at the stars.

This feeling is worlds away from what happens to Robert Musil's *The Man Without Qualities*, a protagonist who, upon finding himself in a library, is suddenly wracked by the realization that he could never – even by reading a book a day – truly call himself an intellectual, as his entire life would never give him enough time to read every single book in the library. In fact, he calculates the figure exactly: to read all three and a half million of them, he would need ten thousand years! This stirs up a crippling existential anguish within him.

What's more, knowing that it would be impossible for him to read every book in the library – let alone every book in the world – results in him developing a sort of resistance to reading. It is as if the man without qualities wondered: if I could never hope to read them all anyway, what's the point of reading even one? This is precisely the kind of 'all or nothing' thinking that often sways our reasoning and disproportionately influences our lives – and, crucially, it is almost never a positive thing.

## THE BOOKS AROUND US CONTAIN MYSTERIES

### BUT *TSUNDOKU* IS A POSITIVE THING

Meanwhile, those who have embraced the *tsundoku* philosophy behave in exactly the opposite way. Being able to admire and touch the fruit of human intellect with their own two hands – having access to the boundless wisdom contained within those pages – makes them feel part of the flow of time: it gives them the almost physical sensation of living in an ever-evolving world that never stops turning. And rather than dragging them into despair, this sensation fuels hope – a hope rooted in the potential to learn, to know things in great depth, that is sparked within us when we realize that the human brain is capable of building worlds, forging connections, creating perspectives, investigating the present to piece together the future.

Far from discouraging us, coming face to face every day with a tangible testament to what we do not know but may one day learn keeps a flame burning within us that inspires us to keep pushing our limits just a little further each time.

And the thought – or rather the certainty – of still having so much to read opens our eyes to the long and winding road at our feet. A road that we will never travel alone, because our books will be with us.

# How do you feel when faced with all the books you have in your house?

1. **Why do you buy books?**
   a. Because I enjoy collecting and owning them.
   b. Because I enjoy the idea of being able to read them in future.
   c. Because I enjoy the act of going out and buying them.

2. **How do you feel when you accumulate books that you don't read?**
   a. I feel good because I enjoy collecting them.
   b. Every so often, the thought crosses my mind that I will never manage to read all the books I've bought.
   c. It doesn't bother me all that much: it's simply part of how I live my life.

3. **What is your decision-making process when buying a book?**
   a. I let my gut instinct guide me.
   b. I weigh up whether it matches my interests and whether I will read it at some point in the future.
   c. I don't follow any specific decision-making process – I just buy books when the feeling takes me.

4. **What do you do with the books you don't read?**
   a. I keep them in my bookcase to collect them.
   b. I put them aside to read when I have time.
   c. I sell them or give them away because they no longer interest me.

THE BOOKS AROUND US CONTAIN MYSTERIES

5. Ideally, what would you say is the ultimate purpose of the books you own?
    a. I want to own a vast collection of books representing my various tastes and interests.
    b. I want to read every book I buy and build up a substantial personal library.
    c. My book collection has no particular purpose.

6. How would you feel if you had to get rid of part of your book collection?
    a. I would feel a great deal of sadness and grief.
    b. I would feel a smidge of relief, because it would allow me to focus on the books I am most interested in.
    c. I wouldn't care all that much, as I could always buy them again in future if I needed to.

## Answers

*You answered mostly (a):*
Owning plenty of books and building a collection is your number-one ambition, regardless of whether or not you ever manage to read them. You see your bookcase and every last space dedicated to books as a great source of pride. You can't wait to keep growing your collection!

*You answered mostly (b):*
When you accumulate books, you do so mainly with the intention of reading them in future, although you probably already have so many that you could never actually manage it. To you, every last book is an invaluable treasure and you feel that choosing your next purchase is a significant, even a sacred moment.

> *You answered mostly (c):*
> For you, the most satisfying part of owning books is the act of purchasing them. Having a unique collection or choosing books that interest you is very much secondary: the important thing is to leave the bookshop with something shiny and new in your bag!

## THE JOY OF GETTING TO CHOOSE

The bookcase of someone who 'lives *tsundoku*' – as well as the rest of their home – is full of choices. Faced with a sea of books never read, stories as yet unexplored, that person finds themselves immersed in endless possibilities.

Unread books not only contain a secret, presenting us with the certainty of knowing that we do not know, but they also offer us a chance to savour the delicious anticipation of being able to choose.

Offered this intimate moment with the extensive selection on display on the shelves of our bookcase, we finally feel free to consider what we truly want. We might choose to throw caution to the wind, pick up some old, forgotten book at random – perhaps one we have never even flicked through before – and delve into it. It promises to be an entirely new experience, ripe with the thrill of the unknown.

It is never trivial or obvious to have a house capable of truly astonishing you. Indeed, the bookcase of someone who lives a *tsundoku* life is, in many ways, an unknown area. True, we may have brought those books home and squeezed them in alongside the others. But until that magical moment when we finally decide to open them up, leaf through their pages and read them, they will remain a mystery. They will remain knowledge unknown to us, stories that remind us how many stories there are in the world, how many unrealized possibilities.

# THE BOOKS AROUND US CONTAIN MYSTERIES

*Having a home full of unread books means giving yourself the gift of embracing countless new surprises, each one just as exhilarating as the first.*

And it might never happen, because we already have an interminable list of books to read, all planned out in such minute detail that there is no room for us to give in to our passing caprices, but that is not the point. The point is knowing that, if we really want to, we are free to choose.

What's more, we could choose without even having to leave the house, if we don't feel like going out or can't do it at this moment. We could scan a wall of hundreds of books and pick out the exact one that we need because we want to dive down a rabbit hole, following a sudden intuition that will have melted away like snow in the midday sun mere moments later; because we want to better understand an emotion that has come up before shoving it back down without managing to find the words for it; because, to put it simply, books are a balm for the soul, and there are times when they are precisely what we need to heal us:

* A treatise on the secret life of plants can imbue us with the sense of peace we need to get through a stressful situation.
* A stimulating essay can embolden us to act on an idea that has been knocking around in our head for a while.
* An inspirational biography can give us the push we need to make a difficult decision.
* A playful, carefree novel can help us survive a dark period.

Having them at home, within arm's reach, right when we feel we need them, means that our books are able to speak to us, advise us, help us, with no middlemen or distractions, in the here and now.

積ん読 – TSUNDOKU

In Japanese, the expression *ichigo-ichie* (一期一会) – borrowed from Zen Buddhism and intimately linked to the tradition of the tea ceremony – literally means 'one time, one meeting'. It is used to indicate the importance of acknowledging the value of every single moment in life, of living in the present and enjoying the real treasures: meetings, encounters, experiences.

This inevitably involves taking the time to process the emotions we feel, both pleasant and unpleasant.

Having such a huge selection of stimuli around us, countless sprawling worlds contained within simple pages, at the very moment when we realize we should be in the present, we should 'seize the day', leaves us with no choice but to listen to ourselves.

# 2
# BUYING A BOOK

Whenever Izumi walks into her favourite bookshop, she feels as light as a feather. If she has an appointment to keep afterwards, she sets an alarm on her phone, because time becomes liquid within those walls: it slips through her fingers without her even realizing. The difference between a few minutes and a full hour becomes almost imperceptible. In there, her time is entirely her own.

Her fingers skim across a colourful array of covers, tracing the embossed lettering with delight, and pausing to investigate the most intriguing titles. She plucks them from the shelf, opens them to a random page and reads the first sentence her eyes fall upon. Each day, she fills her head with countless sentences taken from an eclectic collection of volumes. Other people may think they make no sense, absorbed so haphazardly and without a shred of context, but to her, they taste like morsels of exotic foods from all corners of the world. A voracious sampler, she can never get enough.

## 積ん読 – TSUNDOKU

Then she starts to quicken her pace, zigzagging up and down between the shelves and the overflowing tables. She runs her finger over every book she passes on her way around. And at the end, as if performing a dance whose steps she has learned by heart, she stops on a cover and picks up the book. She admires it, but does not open it to read a sentence. Not this time. Because this book is coming home with her. Izumi repeats the same dance twice more and then, with three books safely tucked into her tote bag, she heads home.

This dance – always the same, yet different every time – is the only way that she can feel that she did not choose those books, which now weigh reassuringly on her shoulder. No: it is the books that choose her, every single time.

Buying is a familiar part of everyone's life. We are used to buying goods, experiences and food, and the gesture of pulling out our wallet – or indeed our phone – has become second nature.

You have to admit it: buying something is enjoyable – there's no two ways about it. And, crucially, we derive pleasure not only from the item we have bought (which should be what informs every 'non-essential' purchase), but also from the act of buying in and of itself.

The simple fact is that, whether we realize it or not, most of the choices we make are influenced by our emotions. We are naturally inclined to relive and reconstruct situations in which we felt pleasure, and to avoid any in which we felt anger or sadness. Our brain associates each of our decisions with one or more emotions, which often creates an infinite loop by which our emotions influence our choices, which in turn trigger emotions. That is why we do not always stop to ask ourselves: 'Wait, why am

I actually buying this?' Of course, when it comes to purchases that don't involve any considerable expense, we hardly ever stop to mull it over.

It seems like such a mundane question, with an obvious answer:

* I'm buying this because I need it.
* I'm buying this because I like it.
* I'm buying this because I want to give it as a present, or even as a present for myself...

Upon closer inspection, it seems that all the answers involve a 'because'. This 'because' imbues the object we have bought with meaning, endows it with a purpose, a *raison d'être*. These are answers that look to the future, rooted in thoughts of what we intend to do with the object we have just bought.

* I'm buying a dress because I want to look elegant.
* I'm buying a phone because I need one.
* I'm buying a car because I need to get around.
* I'm buying a book because I want to read it.

We already know that those who follow the ethos of *tsundoku* will probably never manage to read most of the books they buy. They won't give them as gifts to anyone, either. There is something in their purchase that is hard to explain with a 'because'.

## TO READ OR NOT TO READ

Someone who buys a book because they plan to read it right away can't wait to devour the story they felt so drawn to. Their happiness derives from their curiosity about a world that is still unknown to them, from the anticipation that precedes starting a new book.

積ん読 – TSUNDOKU

A *tsundoku*-er, on the other hand, will get home and place that book on their bedside table, in their bookcase or in any remaining corner they can find. This alone will be enough to bring a smile to their face: the idea that this book will be right there with them, day in and day out, from that point on.

But how could that ever make anybody happy? What delight could it possibly give anyone to have spent money on an object that they may well never get to enjoy?

The answer is undoubtedly linked to the sense of excitement, pleasure and expectation that – as we shall see very shortly – adding a new piece to a collection can arouse.

But in our case, each book that we add to our bookcase also represents a new piece of the puzzle that defines us. Not only through our reading preferences, but also through what intrigues us, which differs from person to person and so, for that very reason, makes us in some way unique.

To understand this better, let's take an example from somewhere other than the world of books.

> There are people in the world who take immense joy in buying shoes, even though they already own enough to spend their entire lives walking.

What's more, it is often the case that some pairs are the kind of dizzying six-inch heels that would be impossible to wear in everyday life. And yet, even though those shoes will remain safely tucked away in their box forever, having bought them gives those people a vast amount of joy. Because merely having chosen and purchased them says a great deal about us. It speaks volumes about our tastes. Above all, it paints a mental picture of who we are at that moment – and, more importantly, who we would like to be, and how we would like other people to see us in future.

BUYING A BOOK

Who cares if that future remains confined inside our heads? Having imagined it, in some respects it is very much like having already experienced it.

> Each book contains pages that promise to make us into better people, and each is, in its own way, surrounded by an aura of mystery: a mystery that we long to be enveloped by.

# What kind of book buyer are you?

1. **How long do you take to choose a book before buying it?**
   a. I've barely stepped through the door of the bookshop and somehow I'm already back outside with a book in my hand. Often I don't even have a clue what it's about!
   b. Just long enough for me to read the cover and flick through it to make sure I want it.
   c. I usually choose what to buy before I even enter the bookshop, having meticulously gathered all the information I need.

2. **The first thought you have when you see a book is:**
   a. Great, I'll take it!
   b. What's it about?
   c. How much is it?

3. **When you walk into a bookshop, what's the first thing you do?**
   a. I browse through the new arrivals.
   b. I make a beeline for my favourite section.
   c. I wander all over the shop, exploring all the books and reading their descriptions.

4. **How many times a week do you buy books?**
   a. More than once a week.
   b. Once a week, usually always on the same day.
   c. Less than once a week.

5. **How much time do you spend researching a book before you buy it?**
   a. No more than a few minutes – I tend to rely on reviews or find myself drawn to eye-catching covers.

BUYING A BOOK

   b. A little while – I read reviews online or ask friends for recommendations.
   c. A long time – I do extensive research and often ask the staff in the bookshop for advice.

6. What makes you decide to buy a book?
   a. It's a spur-of-the-moment decision: if it looks interesting, I'll get it.
   b. I add it to my wishlist and buy it when I've got the time.
   c. I wait for the perfect moment so I can get the most possible enjoyment out of it.

## Answers

*You answered mostly (a):*
You're an impulsive book buyer with an inquisitive nature, you follow your instincts (and recommendations from BookTokers) and are happy to give new books a go without too much hesitation.

*You answered mostly (b):*
You're a habitual book buyer, you love following your personal routine and you will sometimes end up buying books that you already own.

*You answered mostly (c):*
You're a meticulous book buyer who makes carefully considered decisions and who likes to do in-depth research before buying a book.

積ん読 – TSUNDOKU

## *Your advertisement*

*Let your imagination run wild: write the perfect advertisement to persuade someone to go into a bookshop and buy a book.*

## THE ALLURE OF COLLECTIONS

At some point in our lives, almost all of us have collected something or other. Postcards, stamps, records, coins, shells...

Collecting has a special charm all of its own, so much so that psychologists have long sought to make sense of our urge to accumulate objects.

The attraction and engagement begin before we actually collect anything at all: indeed, it lies in the decision-making phase that precedes the act itself.

> Deciding, whether consciously or unconsciously, to collect one type of object over another is something that can be used to define our identity.

For example, saying, 'I collect pebbles' is a way of defining who we are and what we care about.

Japan is home to the art of *suiseki*, which is based on collecting stones from various natural landscapes (cliffs, waterfalls, caves, etc.), and aside from expressing a love for the planet we live on, choosing to collect *suiseki* stones speaks of a person's respect for something that is only seemingly immutable – something that is in fact part of the cycle of nature, of being transformed, transported and eroded by it.

In the case of books, the mechanism is very similar, with that extra nuance we talked about earlier: not only does choosing a particular title to add to our collection express something about who we are today, but it also shapes our ideas of who we would like to be tomorrow or what we consider important to us at a given phase of our lives.

What is certain is that being a collector involves a commitment, a perseverance, that means that our choices can never be mundane.

積ん読 – TSUNDOKU

We need something capable of motivating us not only in the here and now, but for years to come.

Showing off our collection to other people feels like lifting the velvet rope and welcoming them into our world, offering a way for them to get to know us in greater depth without necessarily having to explain ourselves in words.

Some people delight in sharing their passion with the world: it helps them feel that they have something in common with other people, enjoying the shared enthusiasm that can come from adding new pieces to their collection and watching it grow steadily over the years. Many couples, especially in the first few years of their relationship, decide to collect something together.

Nurturing a collection is also a way of leaving a lasting mark, a milestone in time: 'Oh, look at that: I got this on that trip I went on with a bunch of people I'd never even met before. I remember when we got lost in that neighbourhood with that cute little market, all bursting with colour and life!'

We associate objects with situations that we don't want to forget, loading them with a huge amount of emotional significance, rooted in their potential to become time machines.

And yes, collections truly are powerful time machines, because not only are they linked to the memories of when we acquired each individual piece, but, when admired collectively, they also remind us of our perseverance and the unique tastes behind our choices, of the enthusiasm that we felt when enriching our collection with that one rare item we were missing, of everything we have learned over the course of our quest to complete the set. They propel us forward into a future where we have a purpose, a goal.

In this sense, books are exceptionally strong 'memory reactivators'. Merely picking one up is enough to bring it all rushing back: when we bought it, where we bought it, who we were with, but above all who we were at that stage in our lives.

# BUYING A BOOK

> *Even if we never get around to reading those books, they move us in much the same way as a photo album, when we indulge ourselves by taking the time to leaf through it.*

Noticing that, at some point in the past, we chose a certain topic that intrigued us, then realizing that it has now become one of our passions helps us to appreciate just how much we have grown and developed, following our gut instincts, even if only by starting with that first book with a promising title that sparked our imagination and set the wheels in motion.

* Picking up a long-forgotten novel that tells a heart-rending love story can make us well up with nostalgia for a time in our lives when we lived in the throes of an intense passion.
* Glancing over certain vibrant book covers with provocative titles leaves us with the same smile on our lips as when we rifle through a box of the clothes we wore when we were young as a declaration that we were grown up and ready to take on the world.

There are books that we pick up again years later that immediately fill us with memories of the irrepressible yearning for change that made our youthful days so euphoric. Back then, however, we gave up on those dreams: it wasn't the right time to change our lives. But what if the time were now and, without even realizing it, the book we had in our hands had built a bridge between past and present, rekindling the embers of what was once a burning desire?

Psychologists also say that collecting objects is a way of exerting some kind of control over our lives.

積ん読 – TSUNDOKU

> How often do we feel as though we are simply being tossed about by the world around us, as if there were nothing we could do to stop the relentless march of time, the many twists and turns of our fate?

Well, in those situations, we unwittingly implement mechanisms that make us feel as though we have some kind of influence over the events affecting us. These mechanisms make us feel more satisfied and even, to an extent, safe, because they are our way of giving our lives the structure they need.

And one of these helpful tools, it so happens, is collecting. Our collections are tiny universes unto themselves of which we can be the architects, the creators, the masters. We can choose what to collect, how much to collect, where to put our objects, how to display them...

What's more, it is often said that accumulating objects is a way of filling a void, and that anyone who has a particularly large collection – which can spiral into serial hoarding – is unconsciously behaving in a way that they believe will compensate for something they are lacking. We fill our homes with objects to distract ourselves from the screaming void within us.

We fill our lives on the outside to fill ourselves on the inside... and incredibly, it works!

Of course, when collecting becomes problematic and the urge to hoard prevails over what was once the pleasure of the pursuit, our wellbeing and ability to live a normal life can be jeopardized. But this is only in extreme cases.

The fact remains that nurturing a collection makes us feel fulfilled, unique, allowing us to stand out from the crowd and, at the same time, feel a certain affinity with other people. We see ourselves as different from anyone who does not share our specific passion, but

BUYING A BOOK

when we meet someone who has made a similar choice to us, we immediately feel a deep and meaningful connection with their way of thinking. Between passionate readers, it can mean love at first sight.

Besides, there's no point denying it: giving up on a collection that we have grown attached to is no mean feat.

And with books, stopping is well-nigh impossible . . .

* How can you simply abandon a fantasy series halfway through, or miss out on the latest release by an author whose entire oeuvre has pride of place on your shelves?
* How can you say no to treating yourself to a new book when you go on holiday, your mind ready to soar higher than ever before?
* How can you escape the siren song of the three-for-two stand?

At the end of the day, collecting books is a little like announcing to the world that we can't stop ourselves from falling in love with everything we do not yet know. Where's the harm in that?

## THERE ARE BOOKSHOPS AND BOOKSHOPS

Is there any better feeling in the world than crossing the threshold of a bookshop? The moment we step inside, we are greeted by the heady aroma of paper, immediately letting us know that we are in exactly the right place. Bookshops are where we can enjoy books as an immersive experience, viewing them in all their glory as a single, immense body before we set about sifting through them individually.

In a bookshop, the sheer potential represented by all those volumes, all those stories as yet unknown to us, melds with an incredible sense of comfort and familiarity. Here, everything we know about books is deliciously exaggerated, becoming richer and more enveloping: their scent fills the air, they inhabit every imaginable nook and cranny, the walls are decked out with their colourful covers, warming the heart on even the chilliest of days. As such, it stands to reason that booksellers are better placed than anyone in the world to understand and embrace those who have adopted *tsundoku* as a way of life.

> Although they offer us very similar sensations, not all bookshops are created equal. Each one has its own distinctive feel, allowing readers to revel in a variety of different experiences. Each has its own identity, its own unique means of enticing unsuspecting visitors to dig into their pockets.

Consider, for example, the differences between the small independent bookshop in your neighbourhood and a large chain bookshop. True, these two worlds overlap in some small measure, but it is as if they speak two wildly different dialects of the same language. And, as such, they offer us two wildly different browsing experiences.

Here is a short guide to exploring the eclectic world of bookshops – who knows, it might even tempt you to make a first foray into uncharted territories!

### Local Bookshops

A true refuge for book lovers, local bookshops are welcoming spaces that manage to forge a special bond with the community of the neighbourhood around them. Often, they also serve as places for cultural exchange. What's more, the booksellers working here manage to devote personal attention to each and every customer,

BUYING A BOOK

helping them to choose with all sorts of useful recommendations – and they may well get to know their regulars along the way.

One shining example is Ler Devagar, in Lisbon. A landmark of the Alcântara neighbourhood, on the banks of the River Tagus, this independent bookshop is a bricks-and-mortar ode to creativity. The walls are brimming with shelves upon shelves of books, a bicycle hangs suspended from the rafters, and the vibrant rainbow of book covers makes it nothing short of a work of urban street art. Immersing yourself in its surreal atmosphere also offers a new perspective on Lisbon and the chance to become more intimately acquainted with this charming part of the city.

### The (Only) Bookshop in the Village

Unfortunately, it is often impossible to find a bookshop in a small village these days. Indeed, a great many village dwellers are forced to travel to their nearest town simply to buy a book.

Which makes finding one all the more rare and precious.

Village bookshops are special meeting places with something of a fairytale quality about them, where books provide the backdrop for intense discussion, exchange and even gossip. They are often the favoured haunts of readers and non-readers alike, because the locals know that they will always find someone hanging around, raring for an idle natter. The bookseller's recommendations take on an almost mystical aura, opening readers up to exploring new genres and buying titles that they would never have chosen at first glance, simply because they allow themselves to be guided by a person they trust, someone who becomes a confidant, an entertainer, a psychologist, a problem solver.

Some of the questions that customers ask the owner of a small village bookshop include: 'Can I throw this laundry detergent bottle in the recycling?', 'I'm locked out of my house, what do I do?', 'I've been called into work at the last minute, can you watch my kid for

積ん読 – TSUNDOKU

a little while?' and 'I can't see even with my glasses anymore – can you read this book to me?'

## Chain Bookshops

For many people, chain bookshops are a safe haven: when you're travelling, if you walk into a bookshop that also exists where you live, you suddenly feel at home.

> There is something oddly reassuring about knowing exactly what you will find inside: how the books are organized, where to look if you want something specific . . .

There is a quiet pleasure to be found in stepping inside and wandering around, letting well-defined categories and clear signage guide you, casting your eyes over the latest bestsellers, then seeking out something new, awash in a sea of recent releases. The staff tend to be reliable and dispense solid recommendations, although you may have to queue up before you get a chance to talk to any of them.

Visiting a chain bookshop gives you an insight into what is happening in the publishing world at any given time: which titles and genres are most popular, what trends have arisen . . . These shops often also offer a selection of other items, almost always stationery and puzzles. You might even be lucky enough to stumble across a bookshop café, where the reading experience meets the warming hug of a steaming cup of coffee . . . What more could you ask for in life?

The largest chain of bookshops in the world is the New York-based Barnes & Noble, which boasts over 630 branches across the US. In the early years of this century, the business came close to bankruptcy because of competition from online shopping, and because of its decision to promote different kinds of products, such as electronic devices and video games, at the expense of books. After returning from the brink of collapse, the chain opted to shift its focus back to books, restoring them to their rightful place: centre stage. These days, Barnes & Noble bookshops tend to occupy smaller spaces than before, with the shelves arranged in a way that allows staff to categorize the books more clearly and, as such, simplify the decision-making process for readers. They feel much more like independent bookshops than the superstores of 15 years ago: three out of ten customers stay in store for 45 minutes or more. What's more, almost all Barnes & Noble shops have a café attached.

## Pop-Up Bookshops

Picture it: you're strolling around your city, heading down streets you know like the back of your hand, letting your feet lead the way as they have so many times before. But at a certain point, you stop dead in your tracks. There's something entirely new before your very eyes. A bookshop.

Stumbling across a pop-up bookshop is a delightful experience for any avid reader. Finding one unexpectedly makes you feel as though you are being summoned inside to peruse its offerings and, hopefully, come away with something new. Guilt is but a distant memory: now there is only destiny calling you, awaiting your response. How could you say no?

Pop-up bookshops are a thing of wonder, not only because of the element of surprise, but also because of the eclectic array of books they have to offer. It is difficult to fit this type of bookshop neatly into any one category, because they can vary dramatically from one to the next.

In Milan, the Temporary Bookstore occupies different spaces around the city for limited periods of time. All sorts of locations – trade fairs, exhibition halls or cultural centres – could be the next stop. Wherever it goes, the Temporary Bookstore brings with it the spirit of Milan at its most sophisticated, offering a carefully curated selection of books on art, photography, architecture, fashion and design.

## Specialist Bookshops

These are the ideal bookshops for anyone who is passionate about a specific topic and wants a wide selection of books to choose from. Whether they specialize in art, fashion, sports, travel, maps, romance novels or comics, the staff at these bookshops seem to be endowed with an encyclopaedic knowledge of their subject, so they can help with most any question, obsession or existential doubt.

### SPECIAL SPECIALIST BOOKSHOPS

The Poisoned Pen in Scottsdale, Arizona, is dedicated to die-hard fans of crime, mystery and thriller novels. It is also a popular haunt for collectors of signed first editions.

Tokyo, meanwhile, is home to Tsutaya Books, which has all manner of art publications and books from around the world, with a café as well as a comfortable reading area for customers.

In Milan in 2023 a small bookshop called Lato D opened, devoted entirely to desire. Filled with books on emotions and discovering our bodies, it represents an invaluable resource at a time when the culture of conscious relating and emotional openness is at its peak.

Pro qm bookshop in Berlin focuses on politics, pop culture, economic criticism, architecture, design and art.

> The store is arranged in a deliberately chaotic manner, symbolically representing continuous change and the passage of time.
> In Ilkley, Yorkshire, the Grove Bookshop is laid out like an old study and, in addition to books, it offers globes, maps and – a rarity these days – sheet music.

## University Bookshops

Hot on the heels of specialist bookshops, we have university bookshops. Often smaller than average, they do not place all their books on display and tend to organize them for practicality over aesthetics. They focus on academic and research texts, as well as course and thesis materials.

Every university is flanked by a university bookshop: a reliable point of reference for students everywhere, throughout the ages.

## Second-Hand Bookshops

The true charm of second-hand bookshops can only fully be understood by visiting them in person. The first thing to greet you is the inebriating scent of old books, which is more intense than the smell of regular bookshops.

These are perfect places for anyone looking for rare and out-of-print books, anyone who appreciates the content of a book more than its cover, anyone who enjoys that vintage, somewhat retro feel and – let's be honest – anyone who loves a bargain.

Wandering through the historical centre of Copenhagen, you couldn't possibly miss Booktrader, a second-hand bookshop home to books in all different languages, bringing a multitude of cultures together under one roof.

## Historical Bookshops

Historical bookshops, some of the most atmospheric in the world, are often found within majestic buildings that are nothing short of monuments to culture. An unmissable stop on a visit to any city steeped in history, simply step through the door to be catapulted into the past... or indeed, into a film, as in the case of the Livraria Lello & Irmão in Porto in Portugal, which served as the inspiration for some of the sets used in the Harry Potter series.

And how could we fail to mention El Ateneo Grand Splendid, a theatre in Buenos Aires that has been transformed into a bookshop? The red velvet seats in the stalls have been replaced by towering bookcases, and even the former boxes are filled with books! Taking pride of place is the theatre's spectacular original stage, complete with red curtains, making it feel as if a show were about to begin at any moment.

## Antiquarian Bookshops

Often small, cramped, a little dark and piled high with dusty old books, antiquarian bookshops can prove to be treasure troves for some priceless finds. The heady aroma that fills them is enough to make you feel as though you have been whisked back in time to a bygone era.

In this case, the magic lies not in the buildings themselves, but rather in what they contain. After all, who could contain their excitement at holding the first edition of a book printed in the 19th century in their very own hands? These precious relics are collector's items to be handled with gloves and gazed at reverently.

Antiquarian bookshops are the realm of rare books, a place where they become objects as precious and enchanting as a treasure chest buried at the bottom of the sea.

BUYING A BOOK

## Kiosks

Wandering around the city, particularly in continental Europe, you are bound to come across a kiosk sooner or later.

Kiosks are the sort of place that is difficult to walk past without stopping. They're like magnets, promising the kind of happiness found only in small things. Think about it: it's rare for a kiosk to be a disappointment. After all, how many of us bought our first books there? Picking up a pack of stickers or a comic as a child quickly leads to buying books as we grow older. Even now, many kiosks still have something special up their sleeve: they draw us in with colourful promises, with a pick'n'mix of paper delights. They offer us a chance to become children once more. We can treat ourselves to the childish joy of a simple, impromptu gift, the happiness of picking up a book with the lightness we felt in our carefree youth.

### THE WORLD'S STRANGEST BOOKSHOPS

In some cases, bookshops can pop up where you least expect them. In Maastricht, in the Netherlands, there are books for sale in a 13th-century church which was deconsecrated in 1796. London is home to Word on the Water, a floating bookshop on a wooden canal boat dating back to the 1920s, now moored a stone's throw from King's Cross Station. That said, it's not a world away from the Acqua Alta bookshop in Venice, where the books are contained in all manner of gondolas and bathtubs.

In other cases, the books themselves lend the place its unique character. Los Angeles has The Last Bookstore, where the books are arranged to form structures such as arches, tunnels and labyrinths, with others dangling high above the customers' heads.

積ん読 – TSUNDOKU

Wild Rumpus in Minneapolis offers readers a little company as they choose their books – a menagerie of cats, mice, lizards, tarantulas, ferrets and all sorts of other animals!

In Nanjing, China, the Librairie Avant-Garde is located in a space used first as an air-raid bunker, then as an underground car park.

At Cook & Book, in Brussels, you can even enjoy a meal. The combination bookshop/restaurant is vast and divided up into themed areas, each boasting its own menu and genre of books.

Last but not least, who could forget the world-renowned and exceptionally charming Shakespeare and Company in Paris? Writers of the calibre of Ernest Hemingway, Ezra Pound, F Scott Fitzgerald, Gertrude Stein and James Joyce have passed through this timeless place, though it has moved premises since their day. Today, the bookshop allows penniless artists and writers to sleep on its sofas in exchange for a few hours of work in the stacks.

BUYING A BOOK

### *Your favourite bookshops*

Answer the questions below to paint a picture of your profile as a lover of books and bookshops.

If you struggle to come up with a name for some of the categories, don't worry: it's merely because the world's bookshops still have countless secrets in store for you.

So don't hang around – get exploring!

- Your favourite bookshop in your city:

- Your favourite bookshop in your country:

- Your favourite bookshop anywhere in the world:

- Your go-to bookshop:

- The bookshop you dream of visiting:

- The most beautiful two-storey bookshop:

- The most beautiful themed bookshop:

- The smallest bookshop you've ever visited:

- The largest bookshop you've ever visited:

積ん読 – TSUNDOKU

- *The weirdest bookshop you've ever visited:*

- *The most beautiful bookshop by the seaside:*

- *The most beautiful bookshop in the mountains:*

- *The most beautiful bookshop in the hills:*

- *The bookshop you stumbled across once and immediately fell in love with:*

- *The ugliest bookshop you've ever seen:*

- *The bookshop where you received the best book recommendation:*

BUYING A BOOK

## MORE THAN JUST BOOKSHOPS

If you want to buy books, bookshops are far from the only place to go.

Just think, for example, what a joy it is to buy an author's book after having heard them talk about it at a trade fair, or how you can fall head over heels for a dogeared copy of an old paperback found at a flea market as you go for a morning stroll.

Everywhere and anywhere has something magical to offer, as long as books come into it somehow. That said, some places are more special than others. You might not be able to visit all of them, but take a moment to try to imagine walking through them: close your eyes and forget about the sofa or train seat beneath you, the traffic noise outside, and picture it . . .

You're walking around Ho Chi Minh City, Vietnam. You are stepping out of the Saigon Central Post Office, where you have just sent a postcard to a friend thousands of miles away. The moment your foot hits the pavement, a sticky wave of heat clings to your skin. You don't feel like heading back to the hotel yet, so you decide to wander around aimlessly, dodging the mopeds screeching past you and inhaling the enchanting aroma of street food. After a while, you turn onto a new street. Nguyen Van Binh Avenue, the sign says. The name doesn't mean much to you, but then you stop and look around. It's a whole street . . . of books! Its entire length is lined on both sides with bookshops, stalls and markets of all kinds. And as far as the eye can see, stacked up somewhat haphazardly, there are books.

You're on a Tube platform in London, having just got off the train at Leicester Square. You ride the escalator up to the surface and find yourself in a pedestrianized oasis in the heart of Soho, not far from Piccadilly Circus. You've come to see the famous handprints of the stars, immortalized in the pavement. You start to

## 積ん読 – TSUNDOKU

wander – not far, just across Charing Cross Road – and somehow find yourself on a little back street: Cecil Court. It only takes a moment for you to realize that you have stumbled across a truly magical place, where any reader could easily lose their head. You take a few steps and suddenly feel like Cinderella on the night of the ball, being transformed into someone else for one brief moment. The thought that the spell might be broken doesn't even cross your mind. Rare books, first editions, classics and children's books fill the street. Merely running your fingers down the spine of one makes you feel as if you have touched a priceless treasure. You walk slowly, savouring every moment, drinking in every last drop of the sheer wonder all around you.

You're strolling along the banks of the River Wye, feeling like a tightrope walker on a rope suspended in mid-air. The rope, in this case, is the border between England and Wales, and you're on the Welsh side. Specifically, in the charming town of Hay-on-Wye. There are very few houses, and almost as few inhabitants: a mere 1,800. But your eyes barely notice them. They're entranced by the books. Books are everywhere, seemingly the real inhabitants of the town, scattered throughout the dozen or more bookshops that are its lifeblood, left on street corners, stacked up on windowsills. Congratulations! You are in the world's first ever book town. Along the walls of the Norman castle, you spy a row of open-air bookcases. You approach it. The books are just sitting there, out in the open, seemingly waiting for somebody. You fish around in your backpack pocket to see if you have any change on you. Above the coin box is a sign: Honesty Bookshop.

Tokyo is a city with countless different personalities. You've come to realize this as you wander through its streets: from the thousand dazzling lights of Shibuya to old Yanaka, the neighbourhood where time stands still. Although you've been here for a few days now, the many spirits of Tokyo continue to enthral and amaze you. You still feel it, as you walk alongside the huge modern buildings by the Metro station. Your heart is in your throat: you've been waiting for this moment for a long, long time. You decided not to rush down here the moment the plane landed, opting to wait just a little longer, so you could enjoy it more fully. One step at a time, you head towards Jinbōchō Book Town, the capital's famed book district. And all of a sudden, here it is. Your eyes are dazzled by the rows upon rows of shop windows, stalls, tables and shelves piled high with books. Almost all of them are used, second-hand, books from a bygone era. En masse, they create an incredible atmosphere of timelessness. Countless eye-catching covers are emblazoned with *kanji*, the characters of the Japanese language, brimming with poetry. You walk long enough to get lost, your feet having to navigate on their own because your eyes are transfixed by the vast sea of books all around them. You can no longer tell whether you've been walking for an hour or five minutes, whether you're still on the same street or have turned a corner at some point. All you know is that, for perhaps the first time in your life, you are in exactly the right place.

### HONMARU, THE SHARED BOOKSHOP

It's right here, in the heart of the Jinbōchō district, that an incredible bookshop has found its home thanks to writer Shogo Imamura. This is Honmaru, the shared bookshop whose name is a play on the words for 'book' and 'fortress'. The project is founded on the idea of creating a shared space that can be used by individual sellers. The shelves are rented out by multiple booksellers, who not only have an opportunity to display their wares for a very low fee, but also get the chance to meet and network with other people, forging an important social and cultural community. As the sellers themselves are many and varied, the Honmaru bookshop is a veritable explosion of colours and personalities, a celebration of contrasts and diversity. Exploring its two floors feels like wandering through a hundred different bookshops. Imamura believes that shared bookshops are the way forward, especially in a world where traditional bookshops are struggling to survive. It's an innovative idea that respects people and the environment, fosters connection, engenders communication and pins its hopes on a future where books will teach people to share.

### *Your special place*

*Close your eyes and try to picture your special place, anywhere in the world, that is full of books. It may or may not actually exist, and you may have seen it, dreamed it up or even merely wished for it. Write about it or draw it, then you can come back and visit it whenever you need to.*

## A QUESTION OF PRIORITIES: LISTS

What kind of self-respecting reader doesn't love a list of books?

If you look through their things – flick through their diary, the scribbles in the margins of notebooks, the notes on their phone – you're bound to come across wishlists of books. What's more, given that we are constantly inundated with recommendations – conversations with friends, YouTube videos, podcasts, newspapers,

BUYING A BOOK

magazines, TV series, social networks and so on – there's no way we could do without a means of keeping them all together!

After all, for readers like us, planning our upcoming purchases is merely another way of thinking about books, the ones we would like to have, or rather the ones it would make sense for us to have, because we wouldn't have put them on the list without a good reason.

> A list makes us feel less guilty: it gives us a rational motivation for our umpteenth purchase.

If we walk into a bookshop intending to buy a specific book, we can bypass all the whims and caprices that usually assail us, safe in the knowledge that we are perfectly capable of making sensible, deliberate decisions. Decisions – crucially – that we made *outside* the bookshop, with a cool head, when we meticulously weighed up the merits of the book before putting it on our list.

In these cases, the steps to follow seem exceptionally simple:

* Make a list.
* Go to the bookshop.
* Make a beeline for the shelf where our carefully preselected book is on display.
* Pick it up.
* Take it over to the till to pay for it.

But alas, experience teaches us that it is never quite that easy. A bookshop is a magical place, capable of taking hold of us and relieving us of any shred of rationality we had managed to hold onto until the second we stepped inside.

The moment we cross that threshold, we undergo a profound transformation. All of a sudden, that scrap of paper with the list of books we intended to buy fades into insignificance and we are sucked into a world in which all our well-intentioned priorities,

積ん読 – TSUNDOKU

decisions and considerations go up in smoke. We helplessly watch the wisps curl and dance through the air and, once they have dissipated, we are left alone to reckon with our lifelong companion: desire.

Desire drags us into every last corner of the bookshop, erases our sense of time and space, fills our arms with books picked up unexpectedly, instinctively, stacks of unknown titles that we didn't even know we wanted. Seconds, minutes, hours whizz by without us even realizing. The list, now abandoned deep in a back pocket, paws at us helplessly, tries to make us snap out of it, screams to attract our attention, because it is the only thing we should be listening to, the only true record of our premeditated reading choices. But the bookshop has its hooks into us, and will never let us escape its snares: it will continue to tempt us with clever ruses, ingenious ploys that never fail.

A half-hidden book peeks out from a shelf, offering only a glimpse of its enticingly vibrant cover. It seems to have been forgotten, a hidden gem that fate has placed in our path. How could we, in good conscience, leave it there alone and abandoned? The guilt would haunt us, not to mention the feeling of having let something unique, something meant just for us, slip through our fingers.

In the fantasy section, a monumental volume stands majestically in the middle of the shelf. The dragon on the cover roars: 'Look at me!' with every glistening scale on its body. We tentatively approach the shelf and pick it up, then realize that it's the last copy. Fortune has smiled upon us, kissed us, taken our hand and led the way. We clutch it tightly, infinitely grateful for the bookseller's ability to make such attractive displays in their shop, grateful that one last copy was left for us, grateful for our enviable luck. We'll skip all the way home with it in our hands, feeling nothing short of blessed.

When we emerge from the shop, we blink at the glare of the afternoon sun and, shaking off the daze that comes with waking from an unexpected nap, look around in confusion.

BUYING A BOOK

> Then, as if struck by sudden inspiration, we fish around in our pocket, pull out the list and scan the titles on it. We look at the bag full of books in our left hand, peer inside and wonder what on earth they are all doing in there . . .

We wonder who decided to buy them, how we managed to come away without a single one of the books we had so carefully chosen and jotted down after much painstaking pondering.

Looks like we'll have to head back to the bookshop right away to start chipping away at our list . . .

## BOOK FOMO

Among friends, family and colleagues, everyone is constantly talking about what's going on in the world, the latest trends, who's done what and why. Being out of the loop makes us feel excluded.

FOMO – 'fear of missing out' – is the dread of not being part of any of the countless things happening around us, of being left behind, of not belonging. More specifically, it has to do with being afraid that we will miss out on experiences and events happening on social networks, in virtual reality.

Social networks can leave their users beset by the anxiety of not knowing what's going on, which largely tends to coincide with what other people post.

It is a unique and exceptionally modern flavour of anxiety: not knowing what's going on in our bubble, overlooking some crucial piece of information when forging interpersonal relationships, ending up cut out of any number of conversations.

So what does this have to do with books?

Well, not everyone knows this, but Book FOMO also exists. That anxiety at the thought of not managing to read all the books

積ん読 – TSUNDOKU

we'd like to – perhaps even the ones we put on a specific list after noticing that everyone was talking about them at the same time. And it can crop up for any number of reasons:

* Because that novel has won a prize.
* Because that essay has sparked a lively debate.
* Because wherever we turn, we see the image of that cover.
* Because a friend, our most trusted advisor when it comes to books, has gone on about it endlessly, and we can't wait to finally join in the discussion.
* Because that title is so perfectly clever that it has almost become an expression in its own right.
* Because the author has had the skill and foresight to incorporate just the right themes to interpret the age we are living in.
* Because multiple book influencers we follow have posted content about this one book, filling us with curiosity and anticipation.

Now, if this were the case for, say, one book a month, it would be more stimulating than anxiety-inducing.

But the fact is that, if we wanted to keep abreast of all the latest trends, we would have to compile infinitely long reading lists that we updated every day: this frenetic, relentless onslaught of stimuli stems mainly from social media, which is the source of all FOMO.

> Already reeling from the anxiety of not managing to read all the books they would like to, the social reader must survive the one-two punch of realizing that they will never even manage to read all the latest trendy books before that trend passes and others begin to appear on the horizon.

BUYING A BOOK

The hashtag #BookTok, popular on TikTok, is one of the means readers use to talk about the books they read, recommend them to others, and describe them in a few pithy words. It is also one of the main forces capable of setting new trends, often managing to help relatively unknown books rocket to the top of the charts. BookTok surprises publishers and booksellers alike, as they often find themselves suddenly having to manage inordinate numbers of wholly unexpected requests for titles that may have seen limited sales when they first hit shelves.

Or rather, that's how it used to be. Nowadays, a great many bookshops have a dedicated 'BookTok' section specifically for all the hottest books that have exploded in popularity overnight. What's more, booksellers have started harnessing the remarkable power of social media, which helps them to cater to their customers and stage spectacular and highly appealing themed window displays.

In short, reading has become all the rage in recent years, and there are some books that you simply cannot overlook if you want people to know you're down with the kids.

At this point, it becomes clear that the issue is no longer merely an anxious desire to read as much as possible. It is first and foremost the anxious need to know what you should have read in order to keep up with what everyone else is talking about, as well as reading fast enough to stay on top of the latest trends, which come and go at lightning speed.

> Poor, unfortunate sufferers from Book FOMO struggle to stop and savour the book they are already reading, because all the while a whirlwind of covers and titles that they have yet to begin is swirling around in their heads.

## 積ん読 – TSUNDOKU

Reading, as we well know, takes time: even the fastest readers among us still have to invest hours, if not days, in finishing a book. And the rhythm, dictated by the book itself, can vary: we breathlessly devour suspenseful passages that keep us on tenterhooks, but slow down to thoroughly absorb a particularly florid description of a landscape. But if we are to consider ourselves passionate about reading, it is paramount to devote the right amount of time and respect to the pursuit. Imagine reading while beset by the constant, bothersome thought that, all the time you are immersed in the pages of one book, you're missing out on hundreds of others. However quickly you race through it, you will always end up left in the dust.

> If you want to tackle the Book FOMO monster, never fear! You're in the right place. Who better than people who hoard piles upon piles of books they will never read to teach you how to deal with it?

Those who have embraced *tsundoku* as a philosophy are necessarily, as we shall see, world-class experts in improvisation, talking about books they've never read and the delicate art of skimming. An approach that allows them to keep up with 'what everyone's reading right now', but *sans* the existential dread.

## TARGETED LISTS

*Helpful as they may be, reading lists can sometimes leave us in a tizz, as we seasoned readers know all too well. There are so many books that we'd like to buy that, when we finally get around to it, we don't know where to start, as it means combing through pages upon pages of lists every single time.*

*So here are a few suggestions as to how you can divide your tangled, unwieldy wishlist into a series of streamlined, targeted lists that will immediately point you in the right direction.*

*Not least because – let's admit it – the more lists you make, the more books you can cram into them without feeling guilty!*

- Summer reads
- Great classics I haven't read yet
- Award-winning books
- Recommended books
- Trendy books, the latest releases, the ones everyone is talking about
- BookTok trends
- Non-fiction related to that subject I've always wanted to learn more about
- All the books by that one author that I don't have yet
- Books I've read in the past when I borrowed them that I would finally like to own – perhaps even to reread them!
- Books that inspired films I liked
- Graphic novels
- Biographies
- Books about writing books
- Books to make me laugh
- Books to make me cry

積ん読 – TSUNDOKU

- ✿ Books containing at least one elf
- ✿ Books about cats
- ✿ Books from the most interesting independent publishers
- ✿ Books with wonderful titles
- ✿ Books you can read over a three-hour train journey
- ✿ Expensive books that I'd love to treat myself to

Your ideas:

BUYING A BOOK

## REBELLING AGAINST LISTS

*What should you do if you end up buying a book that's not on your list? Although to tell the truth, this is less an if than a when. Because impulse buying – as we are now well aware – is inevitable, and as the crushing guilt floods your being, you rack your brain: how could this have happened? What possessed you while you were in the bookshop? 'This'll be the last time,' you tell yourself, but deep down you know full well that you said those exact words last time, and the time before that . . .*

*But fret not! Nothing terrible has happened, nobody has died and all this can be fixed – especially if you follow these handy tips.*

- *Add your new purchase to the list – not right at the end, maybe somewhere in the middle – then pretend it was there all along and immediately tick it off: mission accomplished.*
- *Rip up or delete the list. List? What list? It never existed . . . then you can start afresh with a new one, see?*
- *Repeat this mantra to yourself over and over: 'It was just a list, it wasn't carved in stone.'*
- *Books that are discounted or on offer don't count, just so you know.*
- *The bookseller recommended it, and you couldn't say no just to stick to your list: that would have been a terrible shame, because they've always given you such good advice. You made the right decision. Give yourself a pat on the back.*
- *When you get home, nonchalantly slide the book between a few others you bought ages ago. Remind yourself that no, that's not a new purchase, it's been there for a while now.*

積ん読 – TSUNDOKU

- ❀ Make an unprompted and selfless gesture of love by gifting it to someone else (ideally someone who always lends you books and never bothers to check whether you've returned them).
- ❀ Consider the importance of the expression: 'Rules are made to be broken.' You've got a rebellious, revolutionary spirit. You should be proud of it!
- ❀ Post it on social media. How could you let a silly old list hold you back from offering other people a great recommendation? Besides, likes and shares will always help you feel better.
- ❀ Create a new list entitled 'Books that weren't on the list, but that I bought anyway'. Balance will be restored to the universe . . . at least until this new list becomes even longer than the original one.
- ❀ Consider that, at the end of the day, it's better to break the implicit promise contained within a list than, say, to run a red light, snap at your teacher or boss, go out and wander the streets naked or run out of a restaurant without paying.
- ❀ Refer to the hundred excuses to keep accumulating books that you'll find at the end of this book.

# 3
# A HOUSE FULL OF BOOKS

'Shall I come over to yours?'

Izumi stares at her phone screen. She keeps opening and closing the messaging app, perhaps out of some vague hope of seeing the question change. But no luck: it remains the same.

She's been going out with Sota for a month now, and she's smitten with him. He makes her laugh, and when he smiles his whole face lights up. Izumi has noticed that as the moment she will next see him draws ever closer, she becomes happier, lighter, with a skip in her step. She likes him and she likes strolling through the streets of Tokyo with him, walking purely for the pleasure of it. They could talk for hours on end, but are equally content sharing a comfortable silence. She told him about the many books that make her house feel so vibrantly alive. He said that he'd love to see them. 'Oh, one day,' she replied.

積ん読 – TSUNDOKU

Izumi looks back at her phone screen. 'Shall I come over?'

She has no idea how to respond. She likes Sota, she really does. But 'over to yours'... How can she break it to him that her house isn't like other people's? Her house is overflowing with books. And the problem isn't so much the mess, or even the fear of Sota getting scared off because there are too many of them. Izumi isn't all that bothered about other people's judgements. No: the problem is that at her house, it isn't just her furniture and plants, her curtains and teacups that speak to who she is. Every single book she owns speaks to who she is. They speak volumes, in fact. They are capable of exposing her, laying her bare for him to see, with nothing more than their mere presence. Behind every book is a choice, and every choice defines who she is.

And she isn't sure whether she's quite ready to give Sota a front-row seat to her naked truth. Inviting him into her house would be like inviting him to slice her open and rifle through her internal organs.

Izumi casts a last worried glance at her phone, then turns it off. She turns on the radio, closes her eyes and lets waves of smooth jazz carry her fears away.

The home of a *tsundoku* practitioner is not like other homes. Not only because an unsuspecting guest risks struggling to find anywhere to sit or stumbling across any number of rickety piles of books tucked away in the most unlikely of places. The fact is that any home holds up a mirror to the soul of whoever lives there – but a *tsundoku* home is more like a house of mirrors.

Every home is representative of the people who live there: you need only walk into a stranger's flat and take a quick glance around to learn a great deal about who they are.

* Is the furniture classic or modern?
* Are there any plants?
* Photos?
* Paintings?
* Are the rooms tidy or messy?
* Bright or dim?
* Is the kitchen big or small?

The choices we make say so much about who we are – but they don't say *everything*. Scrutinizing someone's home can offer us fragmented insights into their personality, some of their favourite things, perhaps even some of their obsessions. However, the most intimate and deeply hidden part of them, the part defined by everything they feel, experience and are – in other words, their soul – remains a secret all their own.

Imagine, for example, that you walk into someone's house and find a tiny yet immaculately clean kitchen. You might be tempted to think that whoever lives there doesn't like cooking, or at least that they don't do it very often. Maybe they eat out a lot or order a lot of takeaways. If you look further, you could check whether they have dedicated any of the precious little space in their kitchen to a microwave or air-fryer. And if you want to dig even deeper, you could open the fridge and take a look to see if it's empty or full of food.

If they have a microwave and the fridge is empty, then you'll have some fairly solid evidence to back up your theory. You might think that you have discovered something new about whoever lives in that house. But you can't be absolutely certain until you talk to them. If their tiny kitchen is spotless, they have a microwave and the fridge is empty, maybe it's because they have just finished cleaning, cleared out the fridge as they're about to go shopping, and find that having a microwave can come in handy every now and then.

Even so, you still wouldn't have any idea what kind of relationship they have with food, what their favourite dish is, if they're intending to improve their diet or if they're going vegetarian.

Essentially, certain details can allow you to make educated guesses, but they'll never tell you everything you need to know.

> If you peruse the books that fill some people's homes, however, you can paint a much more nuanced picture of them, because behind every book is a deliberate choice that says something about the person who made it.

Anyone entering a new house needs nothing more than a brief gander around the place to glean a new kind of knowledge: how are the books arranged? Are they tidy or messy? What's the organizational system like? Are they all hefty bricks or flimsy paperbacks? Are there more novels or non-fiction, textbooks or recipe books?

You can quickly understand how even a cursory glance around a *tsundoku* home can reveal a great deal about the resident's tastes.

But if you really get down into the nitty-gritty of it, if you stop to take a closer look at their books, then you will see their soul laid bare before your very eyes. Each one is a piece of the puzzle, a fragment of their story.

What are the non-fiction books in Izumi's hallway about? Animals, technology, linguistics? Are the romance novels in her bedroom tragic tales of doomed love or soppy stories with a happy ending?

Each book conveys something about the person who owns it: a moment in their life, a dream, an interest, a passion.

Are these teetering towers of books all about making you cry, making you laugh or explaining an idea? Or perhaps even all three?

A HOUSE FULL OF BOOKS

> Hidden within our bookshelves are all the
> countless facets that make us who we are.

For those who live *tsundoku*, inviting someone over is like having a guest peer into the depths of their soul. So if you've ever had the honour of entering their home, you should feel grateful. It means that they trust you.

### *The story your home tells about you*

*What do the books living on the shelves in your home say about you?*

*Here's an experiment to try: leave the house by the front door, close it (don't forget your keys!) and wait a minute. Then open it again and step back inside.*

*Take a look around. Do it with fresh eyes, as if it were someone else's house and you were entering for the first time.*

*Try to notice the first books your eyes land on, then slowly start to explore the bookcases, the piles stacked all around, the individual shelves. And all the while, ask yourself: what do they say about the person who lives here? Answer this question as if you were a complete stranger to yourself. What do your books say about you? Based solely on those books, how would you imagine the person who lives in your house?*

_____

_____

_____

_____

積ん読 – TSUNDOKU

## BEAUTIFULLY ORGANIZED BOOKSHELVES

Someone who has embraced *tsundoku* as a philosophy organizes their collection with great care and deliberation. As a passionate serial accumulator of books, they are often exceptionally meticulous when considering how to arrange them.

It is a truth universally acknowledged that when new books keep relentlessly streaming into the house, keeping everything tidy becomes a challenge: that's why bookcases need to be reorganized frequently, not least because it helps to free up other spaces in the house!

Let's have a go at it together, starting with a few simple tips. We'll try to follow a step-by-step method, without being discouraged by the fact that the first few stages will plunge us into utter chaos:

## A HOUSE FULL OF BOOKS

First things first:

* Remove all the books from every shelf.
* Remove them from the bedside table...
* ...bathtub...
* ...kitchen cabinet.
* Lay them all out on the floor.

You're right, there are hundreds of them, but don't let that scare you. It doesn't matter if you can't see a sliver of floor beneath them. The important thing is to take them out of their original spot – you know, that place you stuffed them the day you bought them that they haven't left ever since? Putting them all on the floor is the only way that you can actually take stock of how many you have, which ones are truly important to you, and which ones you would be happy to sell on or give away. You might well end up keeping every single one of them, but that's okay.

Now that all your books are at your feet, the rest of the house will seem eerily empty. Try looking around and squinting to see if you can picture how your space could be transformed, how the books could fill it in a different way. Before you begin, there is one question you must answer:

* *Is my priority to have an aesthetically pleasing bookcase or for the books to be organized according to a specific criteria? In other words: do I want to be able to find what I'm looking for quickly, or do I want to look around and feel a sense of satisfaction at how beautifully and harmoniously the books are arranged?*

This question is the foundation for the whole process, the first crucial choice you have to make. It's important for your home to look good and for your bookcase to reflect your aesthetic tastes.

But at the same time, given the vast number of books you probably own, it is also important not to waste hours looking for that one particular title you've finally found the time to read.

So it's down to you to figure out which need you consider more pressing. If you're really struggling to choose, don't fret: some of the methods available to you try to find a happy medium between the two.

Books can be classified first and foremost according to three qualities:

* What they're like on the outside
* What they're like on the inside
* Who they are

A bit like people, really: every one of us has aesthetic features that make us recognizable, from the colour of our eyes to the size of our nose, along with height, hair colour . . . you get the picture. Then each of us has a personality, thoughts, passions, a certain attitude that makes us who we are. Plus a first name, a surname and a place of birth to tell us where we belong in the world.

You can think of a book in similar terms. It has aesthetic features (colour, format, cover style . . .), a certain attitude (what's it about?) and distinguishing information (title, author, publisher, etc.).

If we decide to organize our books based on what they're like on the outside, so that they help to beautify our home, then the most simple yet effective method is to reorganize them based on the colour of the spine. Having a rainbow bookcase arranged according to the colour scale is a very fashionable and exceptionally striking bit of décor!

A HOUSE FULL OF BOOKS

## THE PSYCHOLOGY OF COLOURS

Sorting books by colour doesn't just help to make your house more attractive: it can also have psychological effects. Incredibly, our mind associates colours with certain emotions. Each one is linked to a different area of the brain which, when stimulated, induces a particular mood.

So assigning each room in the house its own colour can have an emotional impact as well as a visual one. And this is where books come in.

- Put all your blue or green books in the bedroom if you want to establish a calm, restful environment that helps you get to sleep. Or go for red if you're more interested in creating a place for passion that will stimulate your desire and vitality.
- In the kitchen, meanwhile, yellow books can help to add a splash of sunshine, cheer and positivity.
- Orange books belong in the lounge, as they are good for fostering inner peace, serenity and optimism.
- Purple books are an excellent choice for an office or studio, as they stimulate creativity and offer inspiration.

But why stop there? You can let your imagination run wild: pink for sweetness and romance; white for purity, sensitivity and innocence; black for keeping yourself shrouded in an air of mystique. The lesson here is that the value of books lies as much in their covers as in their pages, and harnessing the power of colour can help to change the way we feel in our home.

## Arrange by Height

Another way of creating a sense of harmony in your house is to arrange the books in height order, from shortest to tallest, or vice versa. This is an excellent means of filling even the tightest spaces, squeezing your reading material into every last nook and cranny. Of course, it is also among the least practical approaches if you want to find a certain book easily, especially if you have a lot of books of the same height.

## Arrange by Content

If, on the other hand, you decide to organize your books according to what they're like on the inside, the simplest way is to sort them by literary genre, for example:

* Romance
* Mystery
* Horror
* Gothic
* Fantasy
* History
* Current affairs
* Economics
* Entertainment
* Textbooks
* Travel guides

Every book explores something different, and separating your collection by content makes it easy to recommend new reads to visitors, as well as to choose something to dive into by simply wandering over to whichever section happens to take your fancy at that moment and pulling out a book at random.

A HOUSE FULL OF BOOKS

What's more, the guiding concepts of *feng shui* also suggest that grouping books on similar topics together produces harmony in the space.

**Arrange by Identifying Features**

Last but not least, you can opt to organize them based on who they are. The most common variant of this is in alphabetical order by author, which should allow you to skip to any book in a heartbeat... as long as you can remember the author's surname and not just the title of the book! Or you could arrange the volumes alphabetically by title instead. Otherwise, you could take a trip around the world every time you admire your collection by dividing it up geographically: French literature in one place, American literature in another, Spanish literature somewhere else...

One method that may prove more useful than it initially seems is categorizing your books by publisher, and then sorting them alphabetically by author or title, as this makes them both aesthetically pleasing and easy to find. Why? Because books from the same publisher usually follow the same aesthetic criteria, especially if they are part of a series (format, typeface of the title and author on the spine, publisher's logo, in some cases even the colour of the covers...), meaning that the criteria relating to visual appeal can also be accommodated.

It should be clear by this point that there are dozens of different ways of organizing your book collection, so there are options to meet the needs of even the fussiest of readers.

## A NEW (DIS)ORDER

*If you're bored with the same old criteria for organizing the sections of your book collection, here are a few interesting alternatives. Because the most effective system is the one that you like best – and, above all, the one that makes the most sense to you!*

*Divide your books into some more unusual categories:*

### Effective Marketing (or Bestsellers)
Books that you only bought because they were in the bestseller charts. (Well done, you fell into the same trap as countless others. And no, there was no other good reason for you to buy them.)

### Classics You Will Never Read but that You Bought Because You Liked the Idea of Owning Them
You keep telling yourself that they're must-reads and that you'll get round to them one day. But until then, you'll have to content yourself with flicking through them and simply pretending you've read them (we'll come back to this in a moment).

### Non-Fiction Books that You Bought When You Decided to Change Your Entire Life
These look wonderful on a mantelpiece or as computer rests, plus they make you look smart!

### Somewhere in the Depths of Your Memory
You could swear that you've read them, but you can't remember a thing about them, not even the genre.

A HOUSE FULL OF BOOKS

*Meanwhile, you keep telling everyone that they're simply marvellous.*

**Sacred Books**
*Books that are exceptionally beautiful – so beautiful, in fact, that, to avoid the risk of ruining them, you've never actually picked them up.*

**Purloined Books**
*You keep telling yourself that sooner or later you'll return them to their rightful owner to assuage your burning guilt, but the truth is that you can no longer remember who lent them to you in the first place.*

*If none of these categories tickle your pickle, then perhaps you can try some alternative organizational methods.*

**The Artistic Chaos Method**
*Where disorganization becomes an art and the books are free to choose where they want to live of their own accord.*
    *Careful, though: you need a certain degree of creativity to adopt this method successfully. Artistic chaos is a world away from gratuitous disorder.*

積ん読 – TSUNDOKU

**The Alternative Alphabet**
Match up each letter of the alphabet with a category that only makes sense in your head. For example:
  A as in 'And they all lived happily ever after'
  B as in 'Bricks' (books that are too heavy even to pick up)
  C as in 'Can't remember a thing about it'
  D as in 'Disappointing ending'
  E as in 'Enormous regrets'
  F as in 'First time for everything'
  G as in 'Guide to plotting a murder'
  H as in 'How have I fallen for this again?'
  I as in 'I tried, but I gave up'
  J as in 'Just one more page . . .'
  K as in 'Kitchen bibles'
  L as in 'Love at first sight'
  M as in 'Memories of another life'
  N as in 'Never the one I'm looking for'
  O as in 'Over and over'
  P as in 'Propping up a table'
  Q as in 'Queer as folk'
  R as in 'Rants about society'
  S as in 'Sparkly nonsense'
  T as in 'Too . . .' (too long or too short, too beautiful or too ugly, too sad or too funny)
  U as in 'Unwanted presents'
  V as in 'Verbose volumes'
  W as in 'Wow, what a twist!'
  X as in 'X-rated'
  Y as in 'Yearning for somewhere new'
  Z as in 'Zipped through it in a day'

A HOUSE FULL OF BOOKS

### Hierarchical System
The most beautiful books live high up, at eye level, while the uglier ones live at the bottom. And you get to choose what goes where – after all, beauty is in the eye of the beholder!

### The Literary Labyrinth
Arrange your books so as to construct a labyrinthine path through your collection, full of dead ends and hidden surprises along the way. Don't forget to pepper it with misleading clues for unsuspecting visitors, with tricks to confuse them and lead them ever further away from the exit.

And if that still seems too mild and you want to push it even further, you could try . . .

### The Transylvanian Castle
Eerie lamps, flickering fairy lights, dripping candles . . . Fill your 'castle' with whatever you want, as long as it's arranged in a way that blends ghostly lights with unsettling shadows, so that terrifying book spines loom threateningly around the room as night falls, reminding you that you are not alone . . .

### Room for New Arrivals
See that little corner over there? Sure you do – that space there between the tearjerker romance and the new book on the advent of the railway. Right, well make sure you leave it empty for any new arrivals.

### Annual Dust Day
Dedicate a day every year to dust, where instead of getting rid of it, you proudly celebrate its existence, perhaps by showcasing your dustiest shelves as trophies of a battle you nobly lost many moons ago. The 'Ode to Dust' haiku on page 152 must be recited in honour of this most noble of blankets.

積ん読 – TSUNDOKU

## *Your very own (dis)order!*

*Feeling inspired? Good news – now it's your turn to create your new world (dis)order and make your collection shine!*

Your categories:

_____
_____
_____
_____
_____
_____
_____

Your organizational methods:

_____
_____
_____
_____
_____
_____
_____
_____

A HOUSE FULL OF BOOKS

*Your ideas for that little extra flourish:*

*And if you still haven't got your space looking quite the way you want and want to give it a more personal feel, zero in on your weirdest passion or your favourite thing in the whole world – and no, it can't be books. Now, whatever it is, try weaving it into your collection. Need an example? If unicorns were what sprang to mind, then the result could be a bookcase adorned with dozens of rainbow unicorn cutouts . . . Let your imagination run wild and you could end up with something incredible!*

# 4
# BOOKS LEFT UNREAD

Izumi's house has a joyful feel about it. That could be because nowhere else in the world makes her feel quite as safe, though it could equally be because of the mountains of books she lives with. The books are mirrors of her soul, waiting patiently to be plucked from the shelf and read.

The sound of the doorbell cuts jarringly through the still air. Somewhat reluctantly, Izumi drags her feet along the floor to the door. She doesn't ask who it is, because she already knows.

Her hand on the latch, she pauses before opening up and takes a deep breath, as if trying to stock up on air in case she runs out.

Sota's smiling eyes peer at her through the half-opened door, and all at once Izumi's anxieties melt away. She throws it open, steps aside and welcomes him in.

'Wow.' Sota's jaw drops. Izumi has done her best to explain it to him, but nothing can truly prepare you for the moment you step inside a house overrun with books. He grasps her hand, draws her near and whispers: 'It's beautiful.'

Hit by a wave of relief, Izumi releases some of the air she has been hanging onto. She happens to be rather fond of her home too, and is pleased that Sota shares her admiration.

Then his initial wonder transforms into childlike joy, and his eyes gleam with delight as he starts perusing the bookcases, running his fingers along rows of spines just as Izumi does, excitedly examining the piles on the table and the floor. He seems to dance between the stacks of books with all the elegance and precision of a ballerina, never toppling a single one, so graceful and confident that he could have lived here his whole life.

He stops in front of an unsteady-looking pile and gently adjusts a single book in the middle, perfectly stabilizing it. He moves on again, but stops in his tracks a moment later. He takes a few steps back and deftly slips out the book he had adjusted from the middle of the pile.

'I've read this one!' he says. 'Did you like it?'

'No . . . I mean, I don't know. I, uhh . . . I haven't read it yet.'

'Well let me know the moment you do – I'm dying to talk to you about it!'

Izumi nods, but Sota has already resumed his literary safari. He explores more slowly this time, indulging in a moment to linger on each title. And he has a raft of questions for Izumi about almost all of them.

'What a gruesome cover! Is the story as creepy as it promises?'

'Whoa, this one's super long, how did you manage to finish it?'

'Ooh, this one's on my reading list! What do you reckon, is it worth it?'

But there's a problem.

BOOKS LEFT UNREAD

Izumi has never actually read these books. As Sota presses on with his questions, the realization gradually sets in that she has no knowledge of most of her paper housemates.

At this point, as he stops with his back to her to inspect yet another book, she notices a sinking feeling in her stomach. A bizarre and unsettling sensation that makes her feel as though she's in the wrong place, makes her want to hide under her quilt. She feels the sudden burn of her flushing cheeks and a crushing weight of shame upon her.

Having a house filled with books that we have never read – but that one day, when the time is right and the stars align, we will finally decide to open – is certainly a romantic idea.

As we have seen, it can be intriguing to know that our collection has such a vast amount of new content to offer us, that it is positively brimming with mystery and untapped potential.

However... (and here's the rub): this is all well and good until we have to reckon with other people.

Indeed, the recurring nightmare that besets anyone with a *tsundoku* relationship with books becomes a terrifying reality when there is someone else within their four walls. Suddenly this outsider, this interloper, is brashly stomping through their paradise, disturbing the delicate balance that the books accumulated over the years have so carefully established.

The outsider observes, the outsider judges, the outsider casts a harsh light on our failings, forcing us to justify the cumbersome footprint of our beloved companions. They send us into a spin with their curiosity, their probing questions.

All of a sudden, we are flooded with the feeling we hate above all others, the one we've been trying to sweep under the rug for years, the one that saunters around with its best friend, guilt, and occasionally comes over to present us with the bill, as it has ever since the day we first started accumulating books.

Shame.

### *Tsundoku* Shame

Shame is the relentless spectre that haunts those who live a *tsundoku* life. It clings to the skin like a soaking-wet dress and is difficult to shake off.

We feel shame first and foremost because of how where we live looks, because our house stopped looking like a home years ago, when it transformed into a chaotic, cluttered library squeezed into a space too small for it. Because there are books everywhere – even in places they don't belong. That stack by the bathroom basin definitely shouldn't be there.

True, other people's judgement is something we all have to tangle with on a daily basis. But maybe, just maybe, if we really think about it, we are our own harshest critic. After all, is it not our own brain that constructs our ideas of what other people might think, that suggests that they must be criticizing us, that all too reliably thinks the worst of us? Thankfully, most of the time, these ideas are pure fabrications. But when we come home after a long day, we feel that we're in the right place, surrounded by everything that gives us comfort and joy. We love our books to a fault, even if they invade every last bit of free space we have, and at the end of the day we tell ourselves that it's something to be proud of.

But unfortunately that's not the end of it. Because while *tsundoku*-ers may spend many a night tossing and turning, haunted by the nightmare of another person suddenly entering their house, on the most torturous nights of all – the ones when

BOOKS LEFT UNREAD

they wake up in a cold sweat, heart pounding with fear – the stranger intruding on their dreams is not just anybody. It is a creature of unspeakable terror: the avid reader, the passionate and relentless devourer of books.

Because while those who do not harbour this immense passion for books will merely cast puzzled glances about the place, perhaps cracking a few jokes and, at worst, daring to ask: 'So have you read all of these, then?', the book lover is a different beast. They will enter our house, their eyes will light up, they will shoot a disdainful look at the stacks of books all over the floor – the chaotic mess of forgotten, neglected volumes – and then, that initial glimmer still in their eye, they will do the most horrific thing imaginable. They will stride over to our bookcase and slowly begin to inspect each and every book, one by one. And when they come across one they have read, they will, of course, have to ask us what we thought of it.

> Spectacular, isn't it? It really moved me. What was your favourite part?
>
> Ugh, this was awful — I didn't understand a word of it. What do you reckon the ending was supposed to mean?
>
> The way he describes the landscapes is simply breathtaking. I've never been there, but he almost makes me feel as if I have. Have you ever seen it in real life?

The problem is that we may never have read those books. In fact, we almost certainly haven't. In the worst case scenario, we might not have the faintest clue what they're talking about.

積ん読 – TSUNDOKU

While the shame of having a house overrun with books – provided that you've made peace with it yourself – can be swept away almost naturally ('Yeah, I've got lots of books in the house – maybe too many. So what? I like them!'), the crushing weight of expectation that comes from someone else assuming that you've read them all can be too much to deal with.

> They'll think that I don't actually like reading at all, just owning books . . .
>
> Have they got it in their head that I buy loads of books just to show off?
>
> They must have the idea that I hoard books to use them as decoration.
>
> They'll think I've got a screw loose for sure . . .

Being acutely aware that we may not be able to answer any of the questions that other people ask us about our books dredges up a deep-seated sense of unease, awakening the dormant guilt that we have managed to keep pushed down for so long.

> How can I justify continuing to accumulate books that I will never have the time to read?

The answer is that, once you have vanquished the demons of shame and guilt, there really are plenty of valid reasons to keep following your heart's desire.

BOOKS LEFT UNREAD

## READ BOOKS ARE FAR LESS VALUABLE THAN UNREAD BOOKS

A person's book collection – the set of volumes they have surrounded themselves with – can be seen as an outward representation of their mind. Giving up on expanding such a collection is tantamount to declaring that you have reached the finish line: I'm done, I know everything I could ever need to know, my mind has no reason to go any further. In fact, going any further could even stir up trouble, as tends to happen when we start to question the realities we have long held to be true.

But a collection that continues to grow, on the other hand, is a sign that our mind wishes to keep our curiosity alive, to remain open to engaging with new voices, new ideas. And, crucially, this counts whether or not we ever get around to opening those books.

If this seems absurd and contradictory to you, think about when you buy a news magazine – not a glossy celeb mag, but one of those dense publications stuffed with all kinds of content, with articles on everything from politics to entertainment, economics to society, culture to psychology.

It's rare to find anyone who reads them from cover to cover: like most people, we will carefully pore over the four or five articles that caught our attention at first glance – one of which might have been featured on the cover, enticing us to buy a copy – and perhaps skim through six or seven others, but as for the remainder, we will barely pause to read the titles or the accompanying pictures.

Generally, we don't think twice about this sort of thing: after all, how could we possibly show an equal interest in everything? However, simply having purchased such a magazine already speaks volumes as to what makes us tick and what we would like to explore in greater depth. We could even leave it there on the coffee table, brand new and untouched, never so much as leafing through it, and still feel that we have gained something from buying it, that we felt a push to take action to expand our mind.

積ん読 – TSUNDOKU

## The Wisdom of Umberto Eco

This great Italian philosopher – perhaps without any knowledge at all of *tsundoku* – managed to explain this mechanism perfectly.

When someone found themselves face to face with his immense library (containing a breathtaking 13,000 books – many people's dream!), they would often ask: 'Have you read all of them?' The obvious answer being no. No – not only because it would have been physically impossible, but also because 'read books are far less valuable than unread ones'.

With his incredibly vast library, which he continued to nurture by accumulating books that he could never hope to read, Eco surrounded himself with a kind of reminder of all the things he did not know. All the volumes that made him intellectually hungry and permanently curious, always ready and raring to push the boundaries of his knowledge just a little further.

We may even have noticed this effect in ourselves at times when we engage with others. During any kind of debate or discussion on any topic – be it with a group of friends, colleagues or acquaintances – we are all too often inclined, when expressing an idea or a thought, or offering an interpretation, to entrench ourselves in what we know to be true. We may feel as though our base of knowledge – which, let us not forget, is largely founded upon what we have heard, observed and, in many cases, read up to that point in our lives – is a bit like private property to be jealously defended. And this comes at the cost of being open to truly listening to those who invite us to move in new directions and appreciate different nuances.

The rows upon rows of books that stare down at us every day remind us how much there still is to learn, how far we can push our minds, how much we can broaden our horizons and welcome other people's ideas with open arms: they are, after all, valuable unexplored territory for us, just like the many volumes stacked up in our living rooms.

## GROWING UP SURROUNDED BY BOOKS

A house full of books is not only a wonderful environment for a child to grow up in, but also a stimulating place that can make all the difference to their future. This has been demonstrated by an Australian study entitled *'Scholarly culture: How books in adolescence enhance adult literacy, numeracy and technology skills in 31 societies'*, according to which a child who grows up in a home with at least 80 books will have developed better numeracy and reading skills by adulthood than one who does not. Just think: having a mere 80 books in the home can have a sizeable effect on literacy, technological and communication skills. The study demonstrates that a correlation exists and, even more incredibly, that the higher average skill level reached in adulthood is not directly associated with actually reading these books: they need only be present in the child's home.

Exposing children to books means familiarizing them with the book as an object that exists as part of their everyday lives and routines. As a result, children learn to recognize books and internalize them as a normal part of the home they live in. They develop a curiosity towards them and, at a certain age, are more likely to want to pick one up and explore what it has to offer. Coming into contact with books is not only important during a baby's first few years in the world, but can also make a difference to teenagers, for whom exposure alone can result in long-term improvements in their cognitive abilities.

積ん読 – TSUNDOKU

## I KNOW THAT I KNOW NOTHING...
## SO I WANT TO KNOW EVEN LESS!

The Lebanese-American academic Nassim Nicholas Taleb, in his bestselling study of the improbable, *The Black Swan*, encourages us not to regard inductive and deductive reasoning as infallible, thus making room for us to reclaim a fruitful relationship with the many uncertainties that characterize our lives.

Taleb uses the term 'antilibrary' to refer to all the unread books that sit on our shelves, reminding us of the vast oceans of knowledge that we have not yet absorbed.

Given that *tsundoku* tends to trigger a chain reaction, the more we read, the more we accumulate books that we will never read (as even Umberto Eco himself said: 'The more you know, the larger the rows of unread books'): in other words, our antilibrary.

It is as if knowledge not only automatically attracts more knowledge, but also opens our eyes to the realization that, even if we spent every last hour of our existence drinking in knowledge with the thirst of a thousand fishes, that knowledge would never suffice. It would always be a pitiful speck in the vast universe of things that are theoretically possible to learn. But paradoxically, the moment we become aware of this, our reaction is not the most obvious one: we do not lose hope or surrender, nor do we stop buying and reading books 'because it's pointless anyway'. No. Instead, we seek to surround ourselves with all that knowledge we will never absorb. In fact, we go so far as to fill our homes with it.

Not least because a book we have read will never be as intriguing as one we have not, which is filled with mysteries.

If you think about it, it's a way of saying that Socrates was right. A *tsundoku* home is a bricks-and-mortar manifesto that shouts at the top of its lungs: 'I know that I know nothing.' I am so completely and utterly certain of it that I want concrete, tangible proof.

> I know that I know nothing, but I love
> surrounding myself with knowledge.
> And bear in mind that 'knowledge' here
> means so much more than just book
> smarts, the facts and figures filling
> textbooks and almanacs.

Some people fill their homes with detective novels, love stories, psychological thrillers . . . and the result is very much the same. Our limited knowledge pertains not only to the nuts and bolts of 'how the world works', but also to the stories that *inhabit* it, the human dramas that play out over millions upon millions of pages.

The more stories we read, the more acutely aware we become that we could never hope to know them all. So if we can't know them, then we'll have to make do with keeping them in the house and having them live with us. We make them the first thing we see when we wake up in the morning and the last thing we see before our head hits the pillow at night.

> Hundreds of unread books,
> each containing its own secret adventure,
> destined to remain secret forever.

Hundreds of words that we will never read, characters we will never meet, emotions that will never sway us. Yet there they are, all within arm's reach.

Nobody particularly enjoys admitting their own ignorance on a subject, but the discomfort we feel when this becomes apparent can be greatly mitigated by knowing that we are always seeking to expand the knowledge we have. And the books we purchase are solid proof of this in paper and ink: yes, we admit our ignorance, but at the same time we declare our yearning to remedy it as soon as we possibly can. That alone is an excellent reason not to feel ashamed of all the books we have bought and may never read.

But there's more to it than that.

## THE ART OF LEAFING THROUGH

Umberto Eco staunchly believed that everyone should endeavour to stuff their bookcase with as many books as possible on the topics they were least familiar with, on a vast array of different subjects, on all the things they wanted to learn about. And in his view, if those books had been sitting around for years and years, gathering dust and never being read, then at a certain point, it was as if you had actually read them.

This is a process that occurs much more frequently than you might think, though you often completely fail to notice it.

How, you might ask? Well, one day, you might happen to pick up a book that has been neglected for years, end up reading a few pages of it, and realize to your amazement that you already know what it says, as if you had already read it.

It's an unusual experience that may yet seem familiar to some, making you doubt your own memory: have I actually read this book and completely forgotten about it? (We'll come back to this, too.)

In fact, there is more than one explanation for this phenomenon, which can be seemingly indistinguishable from magic.

> First of all, you need to consider the fact that that book has 'lived' in your house with you for a good long while, so you will undoubtedly have picked it up every now and again, whether simply to dust it or during one of those times when you were reorganizing your collection.

You may think that you did so in a purely mechanical way, but it is exceptionally rare for anyone to hold a book in their hands without it resulting in some minuscule transfer of information, even if only by osmosis: if you paused to look at it when you moved it, if you noticed a detail on the cover or read a few lines of the blurb, even if you only opened it to inhale the intoxicating aroma of the paper, but then couldn't help but notice that it was printed in a particular font or that its paragraphs had attention-grabbing titles . . . well, then its content has already seeped into your brain and been absorbed without you realizing it.

What's more, no book is an island – quite the opposite, in fact: they are always related and interlinked in some way or other, meaning you can start from a single book and travel to a library halfway across the world by way of cross-references alone. In theory, you could even limit yourself to knowing the connections between various books, where they fit in the overarching pool of all books, and still be able to claim a certain familiarity with their content.

This sort of 'big picture' knowledge also creates expectations for the text – expectations that you may have had when you first bought it, leading you to subconsciously insert that book into a group of similar ones that you have read.

Because generally speaking, nothing exists in a vacuum: it's quite possible that:

* . . . you once read a book from the same series, and it may well have mentioned the very book you have in your hands right now.
* Or you may just have read an article about it.
* You may have caught a passing comment from someone who was discussing it in the course of conversation.
* The story it tells could easily be part of a collection of similar stories.

But that's not all: if, rather than merely picking up the book in question for a moment, you took it and sat down on the sofa for half an hour to examine it more closely, you may – albeit perhaps unconsciously – have engaged in the art of leafing through.

Those who spend their lives rubbing shoulders with books tend to be more familiar with their internal rules, giving them the uncanny ability to glean their overall gist with nothing more than a passing flick through – or, in some cases, just by reading the contents page.

The act of leafing through can be understood in the standard sense, namely skimming through the book from beginning to end, pausing to absorb certain passages and gleefully skipping over others until you reach the end. However, some may opt for a more chaotic method, hopping around every which way – perhaps even starting at the end – and independently reconstructing the author's intended journey.

As such, it is quite possible that, at some point during a conversation, something inexplicably unusual has happened to you. Someone may have brought up a certain topic and your mind immediately made the link with a specific book from your collection. You may have quoted it, talked about it, offered examples and even established connections with other works, only to realize later that you had never read that book, or indeed the other titles you were discussing – at least, not in the traditional sense of 'reading a book'.

Instead, you have quite simply absorbed it into your being.

In *How to Talk about Books You Haven't Read*, the French author Pierre Bayard explains the beauty and importance of not reading books. He even ventures so far as to claim that it is only by not reading a book that we can truly pay testament to the immense love we have for books: reading one, after all, would be tantamount to making a choice, and consequently not choosing all the other books populating the world's bookshelves. The only

BOOKS LEFT UNREAD

way to love all books equally is not to read them at all. Not a single one.

Seems a wonderfully effective balm against all that gnawing guilt, doesn't it?

> Besides, a book we have read will never be as intriguing as one we have not.

This approach allows us the opportunity to imagine the book exactly the way we would like it to be. You could even go so far as to write a passionate review, just as you might in a reading journal, whether physical or digital, and include it in your own personal *Tsundoku Journal of Unread Books*. (If you fancy giving this a whirl, you'll find questionnaires at the end of this book which you can fill in so you can finally let your imagination run riot and put your years of experience as a reader to good use.)

Essentially, you can find whatever you happen to be looking for in an unread book, something that becomes much more challenging once you've actually read it.

Indeed, it is common for us to idealize books that we haven't read yet, filling them with expectations, as we do with relationships. And, just as in relationships, those expectations can shatter into a million pieces when they collide with the harsh reality.

In some cases, you may have set the bar too high – and not because the book had been recommended to you, or had received rave reviews, or was one of the great classics that had been on your list since time immemorial, or even because it had gone viral on social media.

No. Your disappointment is rooted solely in the fact that the book you just closed was, quite simply, very different from the way you had spent so long imagining it. You had painted a certain picture of it in your head based on whatever had first grabbed your attention: the style of the cover, perhaps, or that one sentence that you loved so much when you saw it quoted, leaving it pinging around in your head for weeks after. Page after page, it became ever clearer that any trace of the plot and style you were so breathlessly expecting – that you had prepared for and anticipated with so much excitement – was falling away, transforming into something completely different that blindsided you, perhaps even turning you off the book entirely.

You secretly think to yourself that the book you had conjured up in your mind was much more enjoyable, and that it would have been a better idea to hold on to your imaginary version rather than opening the real thing and shattering the illusion.

Apologies for the reality check: there is nothing objective about your opinion. There was nothing wrong with that book at all, and it may well have been a fantastic read. However, the fact remains that the world you encountered when you delved into its pages covered only the tiniest fraction of what you had built up in your head before you even opened it.

Perhaps that's why Oscar Wilde once said: 'I never read a book I must review; it prejudices you so.'

### IF I DON'T LIKE IT, CAN I JUST GIVE UP?

There's no point beating around the bush: as readers, we have to make our peace with the guilt that can assail us. Of course, we feel guilty not only because we buy so many books, the majority of which we don't even read, but also because of the books we do happen to be reading at any given moment. Because the act of reading in itself opens up the very real possibility that something could go wrong, and that is a possibility we must gracefully accept as part and parcel of the whole undertaking.

- Maybe you're not as interested in the subject as you thought.
- Maybe the story failed to grab your attention.
- Maybe the language the author uses is like nails on a chalkboard to you.
- Maybe the setting is too far-flung and alien for you.

Essentially, you're nearly halfway through and can't stomach another page.

What's the right thing to do? Torment yourself by bravely soldiering on through to the end or calmly close the book and move on?

Many people consider it an affront – to the author, if not to the book itself – to abandon a literary endeavour partway through. It can be tempting to almost imagine that the book has feelings which could be hurt by our rejection. Not finishing it also feels like an insult to the reading community as a whole, the scandalous breaking of an unwritten rule. But here's the good news: there is no rule that says you have to finish reading a book at all costs, even the most lauded ones.

We are not duty bound to finish every single book we start. What's more, as another French author, Daniel Pennac, writes, it is our inalienable right to leave any book we are not enjoying half-read. If we find a book too boring, scary or disturbing, there's nothing to stop us from parting ways and putting it back in our bookcase, perhaps tucked away in some hidden corner.

We should never feel guilty about the stories we don't finish because we don't want to; that said, however, we *should* feel guilty about all the spectacular books that sit there waiting for us to finally escape from our abusive relationship with a book we hate.

## 積ん読 – TSUNDOKU

We can never hope to read every story in the world in the single lifetime afforded to us, so it is truly absurd to waste time on the ones we don't like.

It may come as a surprise to realize that we are well within our rights not to enjoy a book even if it's a world-renowned masterpiece, a trusted advisor recommended it to us, or one of our favourite authors wrote it. But admitting that it failed to captivate us and opting to cut our losses early on need not be a frightening prospect. It doesn't mean that we're doing anything wrong. These things happen. So why continue to suffer needlessly in silence, especially with all the wonderful books in the world (and our bookcases)?

Let's take it as an opportunity to hone our critical spirit by striving to identify the reason we are abandoning the book in question: a valuable exercise that will refine our tastes, offer us guidance for future purchases and, above all, give us the push we need to stomp out the nagging voice of guilt that so often creeps in!

BOOKS LEFT UNREAD

***Foolproof techniques for pretending to answer people's questions and tackling the shame of not having read a book***

- *An excellent approach for fiction is to split books into categories: the crime novels with a tragic ending go over here, the ones with a twist ending go over there, and the ones whose ending you can see coming halfway through all the way over there. One bookshelf dedicated to books with ultra-tense fight scenes, another for books with tight dialogue . . . That way, you'll always have something to fall back on!*
- *Tread carefully: this comes with the risk that an observant bibliophile might pick up on one or two bizarre coincidences when they start meticulously sifting through your collection, leaving you forced to explain precisely why so many of your books feature a main character who dies within the first 50 pages.*
- *For non-fiction, it's worth picking a few random samples, sprinkling them here and there throughout your bookcase, then reading a few reviews online and sticking Post-It notes with keywords only you can understand inside them. When the intruding bibliophile inevitably asks you what you think of the book, pull it out of the bookcase and pretend to leaf through it as you secretly look for your expertly hidden crib notes. And if, by some misfortune, they happen to skip over every single one of your craftily planted books, you can always steer the conversation*

積ん読 – TSUNDOKU

*in the right direction:* 'Yeah, definitely, I completely agree with you, but that reminds me of . . .'

- *Draw impactful-sounding comparisons that mean absolutely nothing, but that, so as to save face, the bibliophile will never ask you to explain. Here are a few examples:* 'It led me to finally understand that yes, fields may be green and the sky may be blue, but in another, truer sense, blades of grass are yellow and clouds are white'; 'The protagonist struck me as a tiny fish constantly swimming backwards'; 'It made me feel like water poured into a vase from a slightly yellowed glass bottle, you know?'
- *Use the cunning trick of saying something like:* 'Well, I have my thoughts on the matter, but I prefer not to influence others, especially when it comes to books. I believe that every book speaks to each of us in a different way, and that's beautiful. I'd never dare to spoil that magic by inflicting my opinion on you.'
- *If you feel like you're really backed into a corner, simply point out that there must be a reason why the first of Daniel Pennac's ten 'Rights of the Reader' is the right to not read!*

# How capable are you of bluffing about a book you've never read or a subject you have no idea about?

1. You're stuck in the middle of a conversation about a topic you don't know the first thing about. What do you do?
   a. I quickly and carefully (so nobody notices) look for information online to get a better picture of the subject at hand.
   b. I pretend to know loads about it, blustering my way through with false confidence and generic phrases that could apply to anything.
   c. I plainly admit that I know nothing about it and listen to what other people have to say.

2. You find yourself trapped in a maze with no map or clues as to how to escape. What do you do?
   a. I use logic. I start exploring and leave breadcrumbs along the way to remind me of which routes I've already tried.
   b. I rely on my instinct and decide where to go based on gut feeling alone. Sooner or later I'll find the exit!
   c. I sit and wait. Someone will eventually realize that I'm missing and come looking for me.

3. Some of your theatre geek friends organize an evening that promises to be 'out of the ordinary', telling you only that you'll have to act. What do you do?
   a. I research and study. I look for tips online, watch videos of actors improvising, and jot down all the great ideas that come to mind.
   b. Great news: I love acting! I eagerly await the many surprises that the evening has in store for me.
   c. I immediately find an excuse to wriggle out of the situation. I only enjoy the theatre from a seat in the stalls.

4. You've organized a pizza dinner with friends, but when you get to the restaurant, you find it's closed. What do you do?
   a. I whip out my phone and see if there are any suitable alternatives nearby. I make a few calls and, if I don't get a positive response, I tell everyone that it'd be best if we all just went home and tried again another time.
   b. I wait for everyone to arrive, then suggest that we take a little stroll around the local area: we're sure to find somewhere that's open for dinner. Worst case scenario, we can always sit in the park and order a takeaway.
   c. We should probably reschedule: there must have been a reason we chose this place, so it's not worth settling for a pale imitation.

5. What's your favourite board game?
   a. Risk.
   b. Pictionary.
   c. Trivial Pursuit.

6. You have to plan for an upcoming trip. What do you do?
   a. I buy a guidebook for my destination and read up as much as possible. I want to be ready for anything life might throw at me!
   b. I only plan out the first few days of the trip, that way there's room for me to be surprised by the place I'm visiting and change my plans accordingly.
   c. I outsource the whole thing to a travel agent: it's far more reliable and not as much work for me.

7. You're about to set off on a long hike. Your backpack is full, but there's still room to squeeze in one last thing. The remaining options are a length of rope and a notebook with a pen. What do you pack?
   a. No question about it: the rope. It might well come in handy in a sticky situation.
   b. The notebook and pen. They're absolute essentials for any kind of journey, so I can write down everything I see, feel and think.
   c. Neither of them. I have to keep it light if I'm walking all day, so I only pack the essentials.

## Answers

*You answered mostly (a):*
To you, improvising means using logic. If you want to talk about a book you've never read, you have to do a little research first. You don't like leaving things to chance and would never dream of giving any information you're not sure of.

*You answered mostly (b):*
You're a creative soul. In your eyes, improvisation has no secrets or tricks, no rules or limitations: it is simply the way you approach life most of the time. You not only enjoy talking about a book you haven't read, you see it as an opportunity to give your imagination free rein and, who knows, maybe even come up with something wonderful!

積ん読 – TSUNDOKU

*You answered mostly (c):*
'Improvise' is a verb that is not part of your vocabulary. You prefer not to beat around the bush: either you know something or you don't, and there's no grey area. If you want to talk about a book, you have to have read it, and that's all there is to it.

# 5
# WHEN READING FEELS LIKE CLIMBING A MOUNTAIN

Occasionally, Izumi is struck by a sudden and overwhelming urge to read.

Sometimes it comes to her at night, while she's still waiting for the sweet embrace of sleep to carry her off, swaddled in her comfortingly weighty quilt.

There it is, that powerful desire, sincere in the way that only things that occur unexpectedly can be. It's no use trying to wave it away. Her rational brain keeps telling her no, this isn't the time for it, she'll have all the time in the world to read tomorrow – the night is for winding down and drifting off, not stirring up fresh emotions.

But Izumi is deaf to reason, because a sense of urgency has taken hold of her and, no matter how hard she tries to push it into the farthest corners of her brain, it torments her like an intrusive thought.

So she swings her legs over the side of the bed and sits in the gentle light filtering through the closed curtains. She plants her feet on the cold wooden floor and stands up.

She doesn't even bother to turn on the light, just glides along in the half-darkness, wrapped in her robe, which billows with every step, making her look like a ghost. She makes a beeline for a specific shelf, but when she gets there and reaches for the book she had in mind, she pauses pensively, running her fingers down the spine and moving on.

She slides back through the room, invisible in the neon Tokyo night, all the way to the pile balanced on the stool in the shower. But once again, as she goes to pick up her chosen book, she freezes at the last moment.

This goes on for a while, as Izumi goes back and forth through the house like a tennis ball, trapped by a kind of torturous yearning that can never be satisfied.

Eventually she stops and – finally, much to her relief – picks up a book. She slinks back to her futon, slips under the covers and turns on her bedside lamp. Opening the book up with delight, she starts reading the first few lines. One page, two pages, then another, then another. At the fourth page, she stops dead as if struck by a sudden and shocking revelation. She has already read this book. She had forgotten all about it, but the encounter between the main character and the neighbour's cat was enough to jog her memory. This will never do: Izumi has so many books that she couldn't bear to reread one. She patiently exhales, places it atop the pile on her bedside table, then gets up to start her search all over again.

And on she goes, touching spines and lingering over titles for what could be hours. Every so often, she pulls one off the shelf. But there always seems to be something not quite right

# WHEN READING FEELS LIKE CLIMBING A MOUNTAIN

about it. She knows this one off by heart, she's flicked through that one so many times that she feels as though she's actually read it, she's not in the mood for that genre . . .

Eventually, with an effortless decisiveness that seems impossible after having mulled it over for so long, she picks up the first book she sees and takes it back to her futon. She nestles into the bed, pulls the covers up to her waist, then opens it to the first page. The book feels heavy on her folded legs, and Izumi finds herself checking how many pages it is. Oh . . . over 700? Really? And, as suddenly as it came, the desire to read dissolves. All that urgency, all that pressure, gone in an instant. Her brain whispers reassuringly to her: 'Don't worry, you can always start it tomorrow.' And Izumi carefully places the book on top of the previous one on the pile next to her. She barely manages to switch off the light before her eyes close and she falls into a peaceful slumber.

## PUTTING OFF READING

'Later'. It's one of those words that can make us feel infinitely better in a flash. Just picture it: the whole house needs tidying, you have to clear the table, load the washing machine and you've also promised your best friend that you'd start planning your holiday together by the end of the day.

Then comes a tiny spark: it's your brain simply saying, 'Later.' And immediately, out pours a torrent of reassuring excuses: 'I'll do it in a few hours', 'I've earned it, haven't I?', 'I'll catch up on it later' and other classics.

Suddenly, a wave of relief washes over you. The relentless weight that you carry around by constantly ruminating over everything you need to do is magically lifted. Only moments ago, you were staring up at your Everest, knowing full well that you had to climb it, then you turned around and all of a sudden – *poof!* – the mountain was gone.

After all, who among us can honestly say they have never put off a task rather than getting it done straight away?

> 'Later' is a magical, surreal realm: the comfort of a place, a time that doesn't really exist.

Think about it: when you say 'later', you never have a specific moment in mind. The important thing is the relief that comes from choosing not to do the task that has been stressing you out so much, the mere thought of which left you wrought with anxiety.

Once again, any exploration of what is going on in our head must conclude that our brain is intelligent. As soon as it is assailed by something that challenges it, it adopts defensive strategies to allow us to overcome the obstacle and recover both mentally and emotionally. It is well aware that putting something off is a means of making us feel better – for the moment, at least.

Procrastination is, at its heart, nothing more than an avoidance strategy: if we can turn our back on the problem, look away from the mountain and pretend it's disappeared, then temporarily it feels as if everything we had to do becomes unimportant.

But the brain is not naturally wired to consider the future. It focuses on immediate wellbeing, turning a blind eye to the long-term consequences that our behaviour might have. How often do we find ourselves awake, bleary-eyed, through the night as we desperately try to finish an urgent job, cursing ourselves for wasting all the precious time that could have saved us from this mad dash to the finish line?

Or, even worse, we may have to deal with the consequences directly: procrastinating results in us doing things in a rush at the

# WHEN READING FEELS LIKE CLIMBING A MOUNTAIN

last moment and, as such, often rather badly. In matters affecting other people, this can have unpleasant results: at work, we might incur the wrath of bosses who were expecting more from us, especially if we risk delivering a project late and forcing others to work twice as hard to make up for our laziness; at school, we might have to cram at the last minute and find that our minds have gone blank in the middle of a test.

But what does any of this have to do with books?

If we really think about it, deep down we know that we are procrastinators not only in our daily lives, avoiding the tedium of tasks and duties, but also when it comes to reading. How many times have we planned to start a book, picked it up, opened it to the first page . . . and immediately put it down as it feels like 'the time isn't right'?

Of course, when it comes to *having* to read something, the issue is much more obvious. What better example than the books we are assigned to read at school? We might be the greatest and most passionate readers in the world, but when reading becomes a duty rather than a pleasure, we avoid it as much as possible. We enjoy reading what we choose for ourselves, so perceiving it as an imposition is sure to trigger our demand avoidance and make it feel like just another unpleasant task on our to-do list: something to do 'later'.

However, procrastination is not limited exclusively to books we haven't chosen. It can even happen with ones we've been looking forward to for ages, books that have been waiting patiently on our bedside table for weeks or months, kept there by the promise that we'll finally start them 'tomorrow'.

> It's not always easy to start reading something new: delving into a new book, a new story, takes a little push to get us going.

## 積ん読 – TSUNDOKU

If the book grabs our attention, we soon forget the effort it took to start it. But it still challenged us, and every time we find ourselves in the same position, our brain remembers the struggle.

There's nothing to fear: reading can be tiring for our brain, but that doesn't make our passion any less fulfilling.

We can even end up procrastinating when we've decided to broach the opening pages of a long, hefty tome. Perhaps unsurprisingly, our first thought at the sight of a daunting, thousand-page brick is often to wonder how long it will take us to finish it – something that can make us feel a bit discouraged right from the off. But that's not all: for a reader, embarking on the journey into a sizeable tome also comes with the knowledge that it will become their long-term companion, preventing them from pursuing dalliances with other, less demanding books.

And if that person happens to be a *tsundoku*-er, then the issue only worsens: in a house flooded with books – most of which have never been read – the struggle begins earlier, at the decision-making stage. There could be swathes of books that we're dying to dive into, that we're excited about for some reason, that have just the right atmosphere to scratch a particular itch. But therein lies the eternal problem: deciding on one precludes us from choosing all the others. This – compounded by the fear that such a vast undertaking could be met with dashed expectations and bitter disappointment – makes for a complete picture of the various pitfalls involved.

Unfortunately, stopping ourselves from procrastinating is no mean feat. It is tempting to attribute the desire to constantly put things off to simply being weak-willed and lazy, which we consider character flaws that can ultimately be easily solved. However, because procrastination is a defence mechanism implemented by our brain, shaking the habit can prove exceptionally difficult. When our mind goes into energy-saving mode, it takes more than pressing a button to boot it back up again.

## READING MULTIPLE BOOKS AT A TIME

Some people might think it impossible to have more than one book on the go at any given moment.

But in fact, it is not only possible – it's a lifesaver for many readers. When you consider it, it becomes clear how reading multiple books at a time can help to soften the anxiety of having to choose: you'll be less likely to worry about wasting time and won't find your mind constantly wandering to all the other books you're not reading. And that's not all: opting for a lengthy tome won't seem like such a prison sentence, because you'll be free from the anxiety of being chained to just one book for a sizeable chunk of time. True, it will take you longer to finish each one, but in the meantime you'll be making progress with several.

But what's the best way to go about it? How can you avoid the risk of multiple stories getting tangled into one big, confusing mess? Well, one of the best ways of making this work is not to choose books that are too similar. Take, for instance, a fantasy novel, an essay and a book of poetry: three very different worlds!

That said, if you truly are desperate to read books that are similar – or at least, of the same genre – then one ingenious way to avoid mixing them up is to deliberately divide up your time and space. Assign each book a specific location and never change it: you could read one in the bedroom, one on the sofa and another on train journeys.

In a similar approach, you might find it helpful to dedicate a particular time of day to each book: read one before bed, one at the weekend or during any downtime, and one on the daily commute.

## 積ん読 – TSUNDOKU

> Each book having its own place or time can make all the difference, because – as we are about to see – the environment you read in can influence you greatly, forging memories that are intimately linked to your reading experience.

The fundamental first step is to become aware of what makes us tick. We must learn to recognize the mechanism underpinning our procrastination if we are to have any hope of overcoming it.

We must tell ourselves over and over again that the sense of relief we feel when we say 'later' is not a genuine response to objective fact, but rather a self-induced, illusory placebo. It is our brain deciding to lie to us as a way of making us feel better. Saying 'later' is neither productive nor useful: it is merely a means of conserving energy.

Perhaps most importantly, let us not forget that our brain feels fatigued when it believes it has a lot of tasks – or particularly difficult tasks – to get through. If we were considering embarking on a journey around the world on foot, we might well feel disheartened and tempted to postpone it before we'd even set off. When the task feels too monumental, too complex, then giving up can become an increasingly appealing option.

But luckily, there's a way of tricking our minds into feeling less exhausted and overwhelmed. We break down the seemingly gargantuan project into lots of small, manageable steps. And, by considering each step individually, we get to visualize all the beauty and wonder it has to offer us.

> Have to climb a mountain? Start by wending your way up the gentle hill through the magnificent woods ahead of you, by putting one foot in front of the other.

# WHEN READING FEELS LIKE CLIMBING A MOUNTAIN

Let's not even think about reaching the summit; let's focus instead on the first two hours of the journey, feasting our eyes on an explosion of colours, inhaling the sweet scents of moss and wildflowers, basking in the sunlight filtering through the foliage.

Japanese has a charming word to describe this ethereal light, which is not only a delight for the eyes, but also a joy for the spirit: *komorebi*. It also reminds us to pause every now and again to recharge before setting off again with a fresh burst of energy.

One step at a time – or, in the case of books, one page at a time. Mindfully savouring every moment without thinking about how long the book is or what else we could be reading.

Making lists can also be a helpful tool. Putting together a list of books to read in the short term can help us push through the struggle of choosing, whittling it down to a much more manageable handful of options (and you don't even necessarily have to start from the top of the list).

Crossing the titles off as we complete them can send our brain the message that we will not be stuck on the same book forever, neglecting all others: on the contrary, seeing our progress helps us feel encouraged and enthusiastic.

These lists, however, should never be too long, otherwise they risk simply adding to the noise and overwhelm. Opt instead for short lists containing a wide variety of topics, so as to avoid conflicts. A few ideas can be found in Chapter 2.

## LEARNING HOW TO ACT WITH MORITA THERAPY

Morita therapy, named after its founder, is a Japanese technique rooted in the premise that it is utterly pointless to force yourself to feel good or hang onto the unrealistic idea that you should be able to do things effortlessly. Instead, it is essential to accept your state of mind, regardless of whether you consider it positive or negative.

This is the basis of Morita therapy: the Zen principle of acceptance.

To be able to act, you must avoid lying to yourself, convincing yourself that everything is fine and that you are ready to take on what lies ahead. It is more genuine and sincere – as well as helping to establish peace with your inner self – to accept your limitations and challenges, and the fact that certain situations and feelings are beyond your control. In Japanese, this concept is referred to as *arugamama*: acknowledging things as they are.

Accepting your state of mind, however, is not the same as giving up. Once you've taken stock of how you feel in the moment, you must then be able to take action. With time, you can learn to separate your feelings, your emotional side, from what you have to do.

Morita therapy teaches that making changes is never easy, nor is learning how to take action despite difficult circumstances. It suggests that you take baby steps in order to gently coax the motivation out – and when that happens, it will give you the power to keep going. Wallowing in misery or defeatism may seem tempting, but it will only leave you paralyzed. Instead, try putting the Morita technique into practice by taking action anyway: don't deny that there are struggles involved, but start with the small things.

# WHEN READING FEELS LIKE CLIMBING A MOUNTAIN

We've all experienced periods when reading falls by the wayside. Life hits us like a freight train, and in the chaos we suddenly forget that we enjoy losing ourselves in a book. With a head overflowing with thoughts, worries and concerns, doing anything – even something that we know could help lift our spirits – seems impossible. When we feel overwhelmed and are already going through a tough time, having to wrestle with whatever life has thrown at us, why pile even more struggles on top?

In these cases, taking a break – yes, even from reading! – is crucial.

But if deep down in your heart, you miss reading, you miss books and stories and fantasy, you miss carving out a little leisure time so you can free your mind and let it wander through distant lands . . . then Morita therapy might be exactly what you need. Sure, you're going through a rough patch at the moment – you're worried, exhausted, worn out – but that has nothing to do with reading. Try to separate how you're feeling from what you would like to achieve. You can read even when you're not feeling fantastic, but first you must accept how you're feeling in that moment. And, once you've acknowledged and accepted things as they are – *arugamama* – you can start taking those baby steps. Pick out a light read, maybe one of your 'comfort books' that you've read a million times but that never fails to make you feel at home. No need to plough through it all in one go: the important thing is to keep making progress, even if it's only a few pages at a time.

And, slowly but surely, you'll feel your motivation creeping back in, noticing that it becomes easier and easier to pick up the book and read. Once you've made it past the initial stumbling blocks, it's all plain sailing. And if not, never mind: you can always try again with another book!

積ん読 – TSUNDOKU

## I'll start right after this...

*And if you're still struggling to start the book you want to read because you keep putting it off, set yourself a deadline. Allow yourself five minutes to solve this word search, scanning the grid to find the words from the list. Switch your brain off for a moment and enjoy the distraction. Then, when you've finished it, start your book. You'll have no more excuses left.*

| T | E | R | U | S | I | E | L | M | F | U | F |
|---|---|---|---|---|---|---|---|---|---|---|---|
| S | E | C | O | N | D | H | A | N | D | A | I |
| U | P | A | M | I | G | N | I | D | A | E | R |
| N | V | L | E | B | A | B | E | B | E | K | S |
| D | Y | I | E | A | R | I | O | F | R | E | T |
| O | R | E | R | S | M | O | R | I | T | A | E |
| K | A | D | M | R | K | G | O | I | S | N | D |
| U | R | A | A | S | A | R | M | A | U | O | I |
| S | B | K | H | D | M | A | A | U | B | V | T |
| F | I | E | A | S | A | P | N | X | T | E | I |
| B | L | M | I | W | M | H | C | Z | A | L | O |
| F | M | Y | A | T | A | Y | E | C | S | L | N |

| | | |
|---|---|---|
| Babel | Leisure | Reading |
| Biography | Library | Romance |
| Bookshelf | Morita | Secondhand |
| First edition | Novel | Tsundoku |

## READING AND THEN FORGETTING

'This is one of my favourite books, I really recommend it!'

'Oh, thanks! What's it about?'

How many of you have arrived at this point in the conversation, only to draw a blank the moment you try to dredge up the information you need? Because while you know deep down in your heart that it's a wonderful book, your brain seems to have forgotten absolutely everything about it.

Don't panic, you're in very good company: sooner or later, every reader has to deal with the frustration of struggling to remember something they've read.

We tend to imagine that everything we see and read will automatically seep into our memory and stay there waiting for the perfect opportunity for us to talk about it, just as clearly and accurately as we could five minutes after we finished it. But that's not quite how it works.

Our brain is not made to store information gratuitously, especially if it considers that information as anything less than essential.

Plato was, perhaps presciently, frightened by the effect that writing – and, consequently, books – could have on our ability to commit things to memory: after all, the existence of any medium that allows us to retrieve information at any given time means that we no longer need to carry it all around in our brain. This line of thinking is more relevant than ever today, as the Internet allows us to not only obtain any information we want, but to do so quickly and easily, requiring minimal effort on our part. We should never lose sight of the fact that our brain is exceptionally intelligent, doing its best to optimize its functioning so that it can remain fast and on the ball.

We forget a great deal and, what's more, we forget it quickly: in fact, it takes a mere 24 hours for 90 per cent of what we have

積ん読 – TSUNDOKU

read to vanish into thin air. And the same goes for films and TV series.

But there is a detail that bears clarifying – one that is sure to lift our spirits. That 90 per cent refers to solid information, such as words printed on paper or the frames of a TV series. These are hefty pieces of data that would overload our brain if it attempted to store them wholesale.

For example, we often completely forget the plot of a novel.

* What was the main character's name?
* What happens to them?
* And above all: what happens at the end?

If we fish around in our head for the answers to these questions, we usually come up empty-handed.

> Forgetting endings, in particular, is something that bothers many readers: how do we manage to systematically erase any memory of a story's thrilling climax? Ultimately, that's the reason we read a story with bated breath: to find out how it ends.

And yet, upon further reflection, perhaps forgetting what we've read is a problem that we blow out of proportion. After all, refreshing our memory about the plot of a novel is fairly simple, as it stays exactly where we left it – that is, printed on the pages of a book – waiting for us to pick it up, flick through it and exclaim: 'Ahh, of course!'. And that doesn't just go for fiction: often, if we want a quick reminder as to the content of a work of non-fiction, we need only look over the table of contents or reread the introduction.

# WHEN READING FEELS LIKE CLIMBING A MOUNTAIN

## The Wisdom of Vladimir Nabokov

It is worth considering – and we shall return to this in a moment – that this great Russian-American writer firmly believed that a book could not be read, only reread. According to Nabokov, when we read a book for the first time, we are in fact merely moving our eyes from one side of the page to the other: an exhausting endeavour that makes it very difficult for us to understand what the text is actually about. Indeed, he even went so far as to claim that we have to reread a book four or five times before we can truly say that we've read it. It is only then, often starting from the end, that we have the right perspective to sort the various parts of the text into a cohesive whole.

It's a little like learning how to hike in the mountains. For our first few forays, it is difficult to pay attention to anything but the physical fatigue we are experiencing or the path we are following. Our eyes are focused on seeking out anything on the ground that could trip us up, while our mind is obsessing over how far we still have to go, how badly our legs are aching and how short of breath we are. But the more we head back down the same path, or similar paths, the more we realize that something has changed. The fatigue doesn't go anywhere, but we gradually learn to accept it and power through it without it dominating our thoughts. Our feet learn how to instinctively recognize which rocks are stable and which are hazards, leaving our eyes free at last to look around and drink in the view. It is only then that we can truly claim to be familiar with that forest, that landscape, that mountain. And we eventually come to realize that all the previous outings were a kind of training with one key goal: to learn how to lift our gaze from the ground and finally become one with the mountain.

Nabokov's musing is also an indirect comment on what leads us to forget: before we can truly possess a book, absorbing it into our wealth of knowledge, we must first become intimately familiar with it. As such, forgetting can serve as a bittersweet reminder that we should give ourselves due time to develop that relationship, just as we do with people.

But what of that last 10 per cent, the fragments we hang onto that have nothing to do with the plot, characters or ending?

If we concentrate, we can often identify sensations that have remained etched into our memory, an array of emotions conjured up as we were reading. After all, it is difficult to erase the atmosphere of a book completely. That peaceful or unsettled feeling that crept into our bones with every page we turned. The visceral hatred we felt for one character, the burning envy for another. The desire to be whisked away to the place so artfully described, or the urge to slam the book shut immediately, as if to escape as far away as possible.

And then, of course, there are the details. The details that we didn't think twice about as we read, but that quietly wormed their way into the far corners of our brain. A title, a gesture, a line of dialogue, a charming description of a hairstyle or an outfit. Those are the things that stick with us. And, when we find ourselves holding a book we're sure we've never read – purely because we've forgotten that we have – they will be the little reminders that bring it all flooding back the moment we embark on that adventure once more:

* The author's habit of peppering their writing with 'anyway', or never using full stops, or the brusque feel of their short, sharp sentences.
* The fact that the main character lives in a house painted sky blue from top to bottom.
* The evocative description of a forest at night.

These are all elements that we notice on some level and that are all waiting for the right moment to resurface.

Of course, it would also be easy to overlook the fact that when we read, we are physically immersed in an environment that will necessarily influence our reading experience. Indeed, the memories we construct around the experience of a book are not solely affected by the black-and-white contents of that book, nor by how it made us feel. There is also a wider sphere of circumstance linked to where we were and how we were feeling when we were reading, a unique and subjective dimension all our own. If we read a book in the teary aftermath of a tragic love affair, it will kick up a whole different set of emotions from what we feel if we read it while basking in the optimistic glow of a fresh relationship. And the memories we hold onto are inextricably linked to the person we were when we first experienced that story. But some factors are much more obvious: reading a book on the beach, for example, with sand caught between the pages and the waves gently lapping at your feet, is a world away from reading it snuggled up by a crackling fire in a log cabin in the mountains.

So we should really cut our brains some slack: as if the information contained in the book itself weren't enough to chew on, they also have to find somewhere to put all the stimuli generated by us and the environment we're reading in!

Let's drop the fear and stigma around recommending a book when we remember how it made us feel, but not a shred of the plot. Because ultimately, that's the most important thing. We shouldn't be afraid of being judged if someone asks us: 'If you liked it so much, how come you can't remember anything about it?' Because we most certainly do remember all the important parts.

Liking a book doesn't mean memorizing each and every word – it means knowing that it had the power to transport us to far-off lands and change us deep down. And the plot? Well, somebody must have scribbled it down somewhere!

積ん読 – TSUNDOKU

## LEST WE FORGET

As we've seen, forgetting the books we've read can happen to the best of us: it's no tragedy, just the way that any normal brain tends to work.

But if you really can't make your peace with it and desperately want a technique to help you hang onto those stories, then here are a few useful tips.

The main factor that affects how we forget a text is, of course, the passage of time. Helping us to understand the workings behind this is a study conducted by a group of Australian researchers entitled *'The impact of binge watching on memory and perceived comprehension'*.

These academics wanted to get to the bottom of the phenomenon of 'binge watching' – that is, consuming multiple episodes of a TV series one after another, uninterrupted, for three or more hours. True, the study might not be specifically about reading books, but the underlying concept is the same. Indeed, our brain uses the same mechanism for binge watching as it does for tearing through chapter after chapter of a book.

After analysing the viewing behaviour of a group of people who watched episodes of a TV programme released weekly as compared with another group who binge watched them, what the researchers observed was that the binge watchers performed better in a memory test 24 hours after having watched the programme, but that their performance took a rapid nosedive over the next 140 days. The weekly viewers, on the other hand, showed less impressive recall 24 hours after watching the programme, but a much less dramatic decline in memory over the next 140 days. What this means, essentially, is that if we power through a book without stopping for breath, devouring multiple chapters a day, we are much more likely to forget about it quickly. Easy come, easy go.

# WHEN READING FEELS LIKE CLIMBING A MOUNTAIN

> *If you want to etch a story into your memory, you must give it time, let it breathe.*

Read the book slowly for no more than a few hours at a time, savouring it like each sip of a hot cup of tea, and you'll see that the words stay with you for much longer.

Rereading is another excellent way of remembering a book, just as Nabokov suggested: on a first read through, we struggle to focus on everything the story has to offer, and the book is unlikely to become truly 'ours'. But when we pick it up for a second time, it can feel like meeting up with an old friend after many years. We already know them well enough to have no need to start from scratch. It'll be a little easier than getting to know someone brand new, and we might even view them in a new light, allowing us to understand aspects of them that weren't clear to us before. This is especially true in the case of books that we originally read many years ago, at a different stage in our lives. Rereading a book can not only help us to remember it as it was: it can also be a source of great wonder and fresh inspiration.

And finally, talk to other people about what you read.

> *Discussing what we read forces us to process it in greater depth: rather than merely memorizing it for ourselves, we have to make sense of it, putting the story or information in order so that we can share it with someone else.*

It allows the information that our brain may have absorbed only superficially to really sink in thanks to the structure and organization that comes with forming and expressing a thought to be shared. It is no coincidence that teachers recommend repeating what you have memorized to someone else as a key part of studying. What's more, if that person happens to know the book we're talking about, so much the better. A simple story told to an active listener becomes an exchange, a discussion, stimulating our brain enough to help it take root in our memory.

If none of these suggestions work, then you can always keep a notebook so you can scribble down a few reminders of what you're reading. The act of writing not only creates a lasting record of the books we have read, but also helps to commit the information to memory.

And remember: if you forget all about a book that you enjoyed, then congratulations, you get to read it all over again as if it were the first time! Would that be such a tragedy?

### A useful reminder

*Here is a template to help you keep track of the books you read, so you can hang onto the memory for as long as you like. Feel free to use it as a starting point for a refresher on every new book you read.*

Title:

Author:

What's it about?

WHEN READING FEELS LIKE CLIMBING A MOUNTAIN

*How does it end?*

*My favourite character:*

*The character I disliked the most:*

*Where was I when I read it?*

*Three reasons I would recommend it:*

*A reflection or drawing to jog my memory of it:*

## REREADING

How often have you felt like reading, glanced over all the books still left on your list, and then realized that your heart's desire was actually to reread something you already knew inside out? Rereading not only helps us to remember old favourites, but also brings with it waves of exciting emotions that may be completely different from what we felt the first time we read the book. Rereading can be a source of great wonder and fresh inspiration.

But why?

First of all, reading the same book at two different times in your life can conjure up completely different mental imagery. That's the beauty of books: the pictures they paint and the feelings they convey are wholly subjective and never the same twice. They're not printed on the paper along with the plot, merely suggested in an indirect way, leaving them to take shape through wondrous alchemy in the reader's mind.

As such, discussing a book with someone else can prove disorienting and make us doubt our own tastes, our own ideas, as the other person might not have experienced the book in the same way as we did.

When it comes to rereading, the issue becomes even thornier: the 'we' we were in the past – who had certain thoughts, felt certain feelings and imagined certain situations – might not be in alignment with the 'we' we are today. This can happen when our life experiences have prompted us to grow and develop our critical thinking, leading us to see a story, character or setting through new eyes.

> Rereading can be a way of taking stock of how we have evolved over time, showing us the 'we' we were before and the 'we' we are now.

## WHEN READING FEELS LIKE CLIMBING A MOUNTAIN

When we reread a book, a part of us is looking inwards, examining our rich inner world, as if there were a mirror in the top right-hand corner of every page allowing us to engage with another version of ourselves on a stage set by the book itself. How many other opportunities do we get to hold a discussion with our past selves in such exceptional depth?

But that's not all. Close your eyes for a moment and picture a place where you feel at home. Try to imagine exactly how you feel when you're there. Now think about how you feel when you reread a book. Aren't these just variations on the same emotion?

Rereading a book is, in a way, like coming home. When we feel stressed or we're going through a whirlwind of change, books have the power to anchor us in a place that is safe and familiar, far removed from our struggles. Even if we can't remember exactly what happens next, all it takes is a certain atmosphere, the author's distinctive use of an expression, or a character's gesture to whisk us back to somewhere we know we were once perfectly content.

> It's like climbing a mountain, following a path you know intimately, where you're familiar with every bend, every stone, every ledge you can cling to.

And if we do happen to remember the plot, then that feeling becomes even stronger: being prepared for a shocking twist, a meeting between two characters, or a tragic death can make that book feel almost a part of us. Just like going back to visit the house we grew up in, or the flat we shared with friends at university. The moment we step inside, we realize that everything has changed, but some small part of it remains forever there, in just the right place, waiting for us to return. And we're struck by a wave of bittersweet nostalgia.

Any excuse to reread a book is perfectly valid:

* Sentimental reasons aside, we might opt to do it because we want to discuss the book with someone else, or because it's the book of the month at our book club, but we can't remember anything about it.
* We might decide to reread the earlier volumes of a saga because the latest instalment is about to come out and we don't want to risk some important detail or other going over our heads.
* What's more, after reading the new release, we might feel inspired to start the whole saga afresh in order to hunt for breadcrumbs scattered through the earlier books in the series, clues to piece together to reveal the ending. Harry Potter fans are well acquainted with this feeling: rereading the first few volumes after discovering the twists at the end opens up all manner of previously undiscovered dimensions, draws our attention to details that passed us by the first time and, ultimately, makes for an altogether different reading experience.

Rereading can also be a wonderful source of inspiration, helping us to understand our own tastes and what we are in the mood for at any given time. For those of us who have embraced the *tsundoku* lifestyle, it's an excellent excuse to buy a new book. We might never actually get around to it, but we can still tell at a glance that it will be one of our favourite reads. After all, as we have learned, it's entirely possible to know a book intimately without necessarily having read it . . .

WHEN READING FEELS LIKE CLIMBING A MOUNTAIN

### *My go-to rereads*

*Time to make a list of your favourite books to read and read again! Here you can finally admit which books you may perhaps have overindulged in. List them in order from most to least reread.*

# 6
# BOOKS WITH A LITTLE 'B'

Houses are not just inhabited by people: they are also home to any number of objects. After all, a house with no objects in it is not somewhere you can live, and it is certainly not a home. You could even go so far as to call it 'soulless'.

Homes are full of useful things, things that serve a practical purpose and satisfy an everyday need: everyone needs knives to cook with, a bed to sleep in, towels to dry themselves on, a table to eat at.

But let's try removing these useful objects from the equation. Try imagining a fully furnished flat, then taking out anything in it that exists to serve a specific purpose. Everything that's left is considered a 'non-useful' object. And if we take a closer look at these objects, really take the time to mull them over, we'll come to realize that, while useful objects leave their mark on a domestic environment because their style reflects the tastes of whoever lives there, it is these supposedly 'superfluous' objects that actually represent the true soul of a home. Why? Because, as we have seen, their mere presence can speak volumes about the person who lives there: they are brimming with insights into tastes and preferences, choices and passions.

They could be a matching set of fancy designer knick-knacks, or a delightful hodge-podge of assorted items: travel souvenirs, paintings, photos, plants (however essential *feng shui* might consider them for every home), cushions . . .

> These non-useful objects imbue a space with a unique personality — often in a more subtle yet profound way than useful ones — as well as offering us a wealth of information about whoever picked them out.

The burning question, however, is which of the two categories books fall into. Are they useful or non-useful objects?

In the homes of people who are passionate about them, they can be found in tidy, carefully curated bookcases that are predominantly functional. Occasionally, especially in the case of particularly valuable or cherished volumes, they might be used as a means of decorating the space, given pride of place on a dedicated side table, some other piece of furniture or a little shelf.

That said, books often also live in the homes of people who don't love, read or even know about them, with many people considering them just another part of the furniture.

Their very presence exudes culture, allowing the people who share the space with them to come across to any outside visitors as curious, intelligent, engaged individuals. Books play a well-established social role, and are capable of communicating a specific

BOOKS WITH A LITTLE 'B'

message to any observer. And here's the kicker: you don't even need to be a reader to be considered cultured – you can simply fill your house with books!

In both these cases, it's safe to say that books have the same sort of value as paintings or ornaments: they enrich a space and tell us a little something extra about whoever lives there, but they are not exactly 'useful' objects.

Their absence from a home, on the other hand, is immediately noticeable.

> When you walk into a minimalistic, well-kept home that is perfectly neat and tidy, you might have a feeling creep up on you: something is off, something is missing. Somehow the place feels empty.

A handful of identikit objects on the shelves, a smattering of bland paintings on the walls, three or four unobtrusive plants dotted around on little side tables. Some people feel that books 'taint' this curated precision: the fact that they come in different colours and sizes can give people the idea that they create clutter and disarray – as well as attracting dust (which we shall return to in a moment). So these people prefer to hide their books away in a cupboard, or confine them to a single room, such as an office or study.

The fact that there are no books on display, however, can make us perceive the space as colder, less human. It makes sense, in light of this, that many bars and cafés should be furnished with all manner of books: a décor choice that helps to make the environment feel warm and homely.

A *tsundoku* home is so jam-packed with books that, at a certain point, they will inevitably lose the almost sacred aura that usually surrounds them and – alas! – start to become everyday objects like any other.

積ん読 – TSUNDOKU

No longer confined to the bookcase – where they maintain their key function as bastions of culture, beauty, stories and pleasure – they start to spread outwards, growing, transforming, becoming every single part of the house itself. They fill every available nook and cranny, every tiny corner they can squeeze into. And after a while, they are even assigned alternative functions.

Their purpose is no longer to be read or displayed, or even to communicate a message.

When that moment comes, the book starts to take on a new dimension of importance: its value lies not only in the contents, but also in the container itself. Its defining feature is no longer the story held within its pages, nor its significance to the purchaser as an object of entertainment, pleasure or knowledge. What starts to take precedence is its nature as a physical object.

At this point, one can only stop and ponder: what is a book? And, above all, what does it do?

Books can be used to resolve all sorts of practical problems:

* Got a wobbly kitchen table? Stick a book under the leg.
* Sitting on the sofa and don't know where to put your mug of tea? Use that pile of books.
* Does that frame on the shelf keep toppling over? Lean it against a book!

When a book is used in this way, it becomes entirely irrelevant whether it is a romance, a scientific treatise or a black-and-white graphic novel. Only its material qualities actually matter: is it heavy enough to prop a door open so it doesn't slam? Is it thin enough to slip under the table leg?

In short, the books filling a *tsundoku* home become useful objects. They shed their sacred aura, they lose their capital 'B'. And so they become books with a little 'b'.

# BOOKS WITH A LITTLE 'B'

Izumi loves watching dust. When a ray of sunshine comes streaming through the window, the dust glimmers and dances. And when the sun retreats for the night, all that dust, tired from its graceful ballet, settles on the books. Books are the place that dust loves best.

Izumi doesn't blame it – in fact, she sees it as a kindred spirit. She feels that she and the dust have something in common: as long as sunlight fills the house, she dances and dashes around joyfully, but the moment darkness falls, she stops dead. And, peaceful and still, she takes refuge in her books.

## DUST

Hated by all, the perennial 'exhibit A' for anyone objecting to the latest pointless decoration being brought home, dust is a permanent tenant of every house, but it absolutely adores anyone who accumulates books.

Anyone who has books at home knows this all too well: dust has an almost magnetic attraction to our many volumes, and getting rid of it is no mean feat. It takes more than an eviction notice: cleaning the dust off books is a huge undertaking, given that the only way is to take each volume off the shelves, tables and floor one by one and wipe it down with a cloth. Then, one by one, put them back where they were – assuming they had a place to begin with.

But is it really worth the hassle, all for a little dust? Is there truly no escape from this Sisyphean struggle?

What if just this once, without mentioning it to anyone, we put our hands up and stopped fighting? What if we only cleaned the dust off a book when we took it out to read it?

But why stop there? We should try to think of dust as something beautiful, incredible, unique. Indeed, we should thank it.

* Thank you, dust, for choosing to settle on my books of all places.
* Thank you, dust, for never leaving my side: you are the only one who always comes back to me, no matter what I do.
* Thank you, dust, for decorating my books with your grey glitter.
* Thank you, dust, for laying down a thick carpet that reminds me which books I've neglected for too long.

If only for today, if only once a year, let's take a moment to celebrate dust and sing its praises!

Ode to Dust (a haiku)

Dust flying about,
amidst pages and secrets,
you fall from the sky.

## MISTREATING BOOKS

*I thought you were a book lover . . . don't you feel bad about leaving them on the floor, or in the bathroom, or balanced precariously wherever you happen to throw them?*

You may have had this sort of question levelled at you at some point, because the idea of mistreating a book tends to make most people recoil in horror (or at least shake their heads and tut disapprovingly). Many consider books to be sacred, untouchable objects that must be kept in near-mint condition forever, exactly as they were when they were bought from the bookshop.

BOOKS WITH A LITTLE 'B'

Indeed, some people only read after they've washed their hands thoroughly, so as not to leave grubby fingerprints all over the pages, and handle their books with a degree of care that borders on maniacal.

* You can't read lying down, otherwise the pages risk getting creased.
* You can't read outside: what if an insect gets into the book?
* You can't read at the beach because the sand and salt will infiltrate every page.
* You can't read while you're eating.
* You can't read while you're drinking.
* You can't read while you're in the bath, or taking a walk, or on a train, or on a plane, or in a car...

Thankfully, this isn't the case for everyone. It's not easy to admit it, but some of us actually *enjoy* mistreating books.

> Our mistreated books are nothing more than the books that we have experienced, the ones that bear the scars of the time we have spent together and the emotions we felt as we grasped them in our hands.

Books that are stained, folded, creased, torn and underlined are books that are real, books with a life.

Not only *can* you read lying down, outdoors and at the beach, while eating, bathing and walking, on trains, planes and in automobiles: you must! What's more, you should *hope* for the pages to crease, for the sand and salt to leave their marks between the lines, for a drop of bright red fruit juice to fall on the paper and a greasy finger to stain the edge of a word. Because that is the only way that, when you pick up that book again years from now, you will remember the moment when you first brushed up against that

積ん読 – TSUNDOKU

page. Maybe you were in the hammock in your grandparents' garden, dangling from that tree that has long since gone but that thankfully left a little resin stain right between those two lines to remember it by.

Those who mistreat books use them as places to store memories, souvenirs of a rich and fulfilling life. There's nothing to be ashamed of, at least not here. Don't worry: we won't breathe a word of it to anyone.

BOOKS WITH A LITTLE 'B'

### *Step into the confessional*

*Here is a free, entirely confidential space where you can finally confess the worst sins you have committed against your long-suffering books. We'll start, just to break the ice.*

- ✿ *I dogear the corners of pages instead of using a bookmark.*
- ✿ *I crack the spines of my books by opening them all the way so as to make them easier to read.*
- ✿ *I use marker pens to highlight my favourite passages.*
- ✿ *I rest my hands on my books when I'm applying my nail polish in bed.*
- ✿ *I read while I'm eating chocolate.*
- ✿ *I take the dust jacket and the belly band off books for convenience – and I don't always put them back on when I've finished reading.*
- ✿ *If I need scrap paper to scribble on and can't find any, I tear out the blank pages at the back.*

*Now it's your turn to come clean:*

_____

_____

_____

_____

_____

_____

_____

# 7
# THE OTHER SIDE OF THE COIN

There are times when Izumi feels as if the walls are closing in on her. It tends to happen whenever she feels as if her books aren't protecting her, reassuring her, wrapping her up in their usual comforting embrace.

She stares at them, terrified, as if they had sprouted thorns all over. They seem to want to climb down from the shelves and encroach on her peace, drawing ever closer and threatening to suffocate her. They make her feel like a prisoner in her own home.

There are times when Izumi hates her home, hates her books. When this sickening terror creeps in, she wants nothing more than to run away, far away, to some vast and spacious oasis where there is nothing between her and the horizon.

So she sits cross-legged on the floor, carefully ensuring that nothing is touching her, and closes her eyes. She imagines being in the middle of the ocean: flat, immense, still, undisturbed by waves or currents. Just her and the endless blue, stretching out as far as the eye can see. Slowly but surely, she feels her breath returning. But she keeps her eyes closed tight. She desperately clings onto this brief reprieve from her home, from the image of all the books cluttering it up, making her feel like an unwanted guest.

When Izumi sits on the floor and closes her eyes, she tries to breathe in a sense of freedom that slipped away long ago. And when she finally emerges from her momentary escape, she usually thinks about what she should do. She looks around and is struck by the idea of finding some boxes, filling them with all the books she no longer needs, and taking them far, far away. She could give them to the library, who would undoubtedly appreciate the donation.

So she gets up, opens a couple of boxes, places them in the middle of the room and sets about her task. She goes from shelf to shelf, from piles on the floor to piles on tables. She rifles through cupboards and drawers, peers into long-forgotten corners. But somehow, she can't bear to cast even a single book out of her collection and into a box. Every time she tries, her hand freezes up. Because although Izumi hates those books, she also loves them in a deep, visceral way. And the idea of parting ways with them fills her with dread. She's afraid of what would become of her house without her books. She's afraid of what would become of her without her books.

## THE LIBRARY OF BABEL

The Argentinian author Jorge Luis Borges believed that the only way to properly convey the sheer immensity of human knowledge was to invent an imaginary library: the Library of Babel.

The Library of Babel is an immense structure made up of an infinite collection of hexagonal rooms. Within each of these rooms is an infinite number of books.

The books contain every possible combination of 25 characters, namely the 22 letters of Borges's imagined alphabet, plus the comma, the full stop and the space.

Combining all the letters of the alphabet and spaces in every possible way necessarily results in creating every book in the world, both written and as yet unwritten.

Borges sought out a way to describe and encapsulate the very essence of knowledge itself in a physical metaphor. To contain all knowledge that exists and could potentially exist, but has not yet been invented or discovered, you would need a monumental space as large as the Library of Babel, filled with an infinite number of books – specifically, a number so high that it could include every possible combination of the letters of the alphabet. The metaphor paints a vivid picture of the immensity involved, of the concept of infinity.

積ん読 – TSUNDOKU

For a microscopic taste of this idea, let's try to imagine that we can come up with every possible combination of just a single sentence. Let's take the title of this book for an experiment.

*Tsundoku: the Japanese Art of Collecting Books.*

Now try mixing up the letters and spaces and putting them back together, in every possible combination and permutation. It doesn't matter if the result is nonsense.

_____

_____

_____

_____

How long did it take you to give up? If you managed to get all the way to the end, congratulations! You must have spent a long time on it and covered far more than the few lines above. Perhaps the metaphor feels more relatable now. Now, consider doing the same thing with all 26 letters of the alphabet, or even just Borges's 22.

Borges wanted to find a concrete form for the unfathomable boundlessness of knowledge, as well as a way to represent how tiny and powerless humans are in comparison.

Those who live by the tenets of *tsundoku* fill their homes with books they will never read: they happily leap into the abyss, at peace with the impossibility of knowing everything.

But according to Borges, there is a bittersweet edge to this: the beauty of mystery and the fascination of not knowing go hand in hand with the frustration of realizing that, no matter how hard we try, human knowledge is ultimately limited.

And it's not always easy to come to terms with that, to live with it and accept it.

## THE OTHER SIDE OF THE COIN

> The home of someone who lives a tsundoku life is, in a way, their own personal Library of Babel: it exists to remind them that they could never possibly read every book they own.

Our books are a constant reminder of how minute we are. And it can be soothing, from time to time, to realize that we are part of a huge world brimming with mysteries that are fascinating precisely because we will never get to the bottom of them. But that's not always the case. We love our book collections, but there are also times when we hate them. It's perfectly normal.

Having to deal with the unfathomable magnitude of human knowledge every day is daunting, to say the least!

積ん読 – TSUNDOKU

### Get it off your chest!

*Living a tsundoku life isn't always sunshine and roses. Here's a space where you can write how you really feel and vent your frustrations.*

## SO IS *TSUNDOKU* ACTUALLY . . . ETHICAL?

These days, buying books is seen as a positive action. This is probably because we associate them with culture, information and knowledge, and so we are used to regarding people who buy books with a certain degree of admiration.

# THE OTHER SIDE OF THE COIN

Our society encourages us to invest in culture, because culture serves to nourish our brains with worthy material.

But when it comes to *tsundoku*-ers, this is preaching to the choir: for them, buying books is an everyday – or at least very common – occurrence. What's more, you don't even have to read the books you have at home if you want to feed your head: as we have seen, being surrounded by them is enough to provide plenty of beneficial effects. Essentially, there seems to be a popular belief that you can never have enough books.

But that hasn't always been the case. It may seem shocking to us now, but in the Middle Ages, the Arabs were judged harshly for their apparently absurd obsession with collecting books. And it doesn't stop there: during the Enlightenment, owning more books than you could possibly read was seen as downright immoral. Who knows what they would think of a *tsundoku*-er's home . . .

Today, we tend to extricate the act of buying books from the overarching concept of consumption, as if they were two completely different issues that could never overlap. But history might suggest that this is a misguided idea.

Someone who fills their home with books that they can never have the time to read is, ultimately, filling it with objects like any other. This is the other side of the coin: it may be considered more rarely, but it's still there.

And it will inevitably plant a seed of doubt somewhere in our brain, prompting us to wonder: is accumulating books actually ethical? After all, books – much like any other product – have an environmental footprint that impacts the world around us, not only because of the raw materials and energy required to manufacture them, but also, perhaps even more significantly, because of their global distribution. History teaches us a lesson that we would be foolish to forget: when the goods we purchase are not essential, they tend not to be compatible with respecting the environment we live in.

True, filling our home with books ultimately means filling it

積ん読 – TSUNDOKU

with objects that must first be produced and transported – but books are not just any old objects: if you stop to think about it, they can live a very long life indeed. Far from being disposable, a book can be read and reread endlessly, and it never runs out or gets used up. The story remains right where it's always been, printed on its pages, patiently waiting for the next reader to come along. The key is what we do with it.

> Let us allow our books to live not just one life, but many: when we tire of them, when we realize that we will never read or reread them, let us set them free to tell their story to another curious soul.

Give a book to a friend, a stranger or a library, sell it, lend it . . . just don't forget about it.

Here's an interesting thought: you might be tempted to think that the problem of book-related pollution would be easily resolved thanks to e-books, but the reality is a little more complex than that. Every download actually has an environmental cost, as it contributes to a cumulative effect that involves the use of a vast amount of energy. And perhaps more importantly, the production of e-readers, the electronic devices we use to read, has a sizeable impact on our planet. So what's the best solution for this tricky situation? Before rushing out to buy an e-reader, let's take a moment to analyze our reading habits. It turns out that, once you cross a certain threshold, the number of books you read on an electronic device can actually offset the environmental impact of producing it. As such, it is only worth investing in an e-reader if you are sure you can make good use of it. You should extend its service life as long as possible: even if it's not the latest, slimmest, lightest, most high-tech model on the market, there's no need to upgrade just to stay on the cutting edge of technology. It bears remembering that when we throw an e-reader

THE OTHER SIDE OF THE COIN

away, even if we don't see what happens to it, it joins a growing mountain of e-waste which is tricky to dispose of and potentially harmful to our planet's health. Finally, make sure to charge the battery using clean, renewable energy. This way, you can be sure that you're doing everything in your power to read as ethically as possible.

As for buying physical books, it's best to start small: for example, consider walking or cycling to the bookshop.

It might feel like a drop in the ocean, but never forget that the ocean is made up of drops – and each of us is one of them.

### SMALL STEPS, GIANT LEAPS

Good news: the publishing industry is taking small steps – which ultimately become giant leaps – to try to make the book supply chain more sustainable. More specifically, the changes have to do with the raw material: fortunately, paper is a recyclable product which can be sourced sustainably. Many publishers certify the responsible use of forest resources, and a lot of them also use recycled paper. They have even managed to reduce the packaging required to transport books, which previously constituted a significant proportion of their overall environmental impact.

What's more, almost all publishers have now changed their approach to print runs. These days, they try not to produce more copies than they can reasonably expect to sell, opting to reprint any particularly popular titles if needed rather than betting on high-volume print runs.

Finally, it is worth considering how effective a tool books can be for raising awareness of environmental issues: after all, discussing sustainability, environmental footprints and waste is another, albeit indirect, way of helping our planet.

積ん読 – TSUNDOKU

### *How tall is your pile of shame?*

*To complete this section, you'll have to take measurements, so arm yourself with a measuring tape.*

*Look around you, wander about the house, search every last corner. You're looking for the single tallest pile of books stacked one on top of the other. No cheating, it has to be the tallest! Now measure it and write down how tall it is.*

_____

_____

_____

## Conclusion
# THE BOOKS OF YOUR
# *KOKORO* ♥

It took her a good long while, but Izumi finally understands what to do.

Now when she feels overwhelmed, she no longer throws books into cardboard boxes at random. Instead she goes over to a bookcase, a pile, a shelf brimming with books and runs her fingertips over the spines until she finds the one she's looking for.

A book that she'll never read, a book she's entirely forgotten about and that she may not even be interested in anymore. Just one.

And when she finds it, Izumi picks it up, slips it into her tote bag and leaves the house. She knows exactly where to take it.

In the park right near her place, there's a tiny little wooden house. Simple yet charming, it has two glass doors and a few shelves inside. It was her idea. At first, she hesitated about even

## 積ん読 – TSUNDOKU

suggesting it to other people in her neighbourhood – she thought they'd laugh at her. But then she plucked up the courage to share her idea and, much to her surprise, they were thrilled with it. They waited for the third Monday in September – the day of *Keirō no Hi*, when everyone stays at home to celebrate the elderly members of the community – and came together to build it. Izumi helped, even though her knowledge of carpentry was shaky at best. Luckily, other people were happy to provide the necessary skills, and together they made short work of it. True, it might not be perfect, but it's still beautiful, with shelves that quickly filled up with more vibrant colours day after day.

A sign above it says: よかったら受け取ってください.

Take me if you'd like to.

There are no two ways about it: living a *tsundoku* life isn't always sunshine and roses. But when you feel overwhelmed, just stop and take a breath. Stop obsessing over the idea of getting rid of all of your books: that would be like thinking that you had to remove a part of your soul. There's no need for it.

Try flipping that coin back over. You'll soon realize that the two sides of it, which seemed so incredibly different at first glance, are actually part of the same situation. One couldn't exist without the other. And it's only if you look at them together that they can truly tell you who you are, as someone who has made *tsundoku* a cornerstone of their existence. But only if you accept both of them. Then you'll realize that yes, your vast and sprawling collection of books might well include some that you don't need, others that you don't even remember buying and even some whose presence in your home remains a complete mystery. But each and every one of them, in its own unique and exceptional way, has done

THE BOOKS OF YOUR *KOKORO* ♥

its part to make your home the perfect place for you. Each of them has made you who you are.

> Above all, never lose sight of the fact that books have a power that we often overlook: the power to bring people together. A book that is given away, lent out or talked about is worth a million other books. It is a book that becomes something else, helping us to blossom, reach outside our own little bubble and towards new horizons.

Perhaps that is the great secret to a successful *tsundoku* life: allowing books to bring people together and forge new bonds, to weave thin yet incredibly strong threads between them, to serve as acts of love.

Is there anything more beautiful in the whole wide world?

積ん読 – TSUNDOKU

## *Kokoro*

*Imagine you only had a teeny tiny amount of space: which books would you choose to keep?*

*Leaving behind the things we love is difficult for anyone, so let's try thinking positively instead. We're not considering what to leave behind, but rather what to keep.*

*Think about the books you love, the ones that are part of you and your home. Think about the books that are a part of your kokoro, your heart. The ones you could never dream of parting with.*

*That way, whenever life dictates that you have to be separated from some of your precious volumes, whenever you decide to leave some behind along the way or feel that the time has come to give them a new lease on life, you can always open this book to this page, look at your list of ride-or-die favourites, and breathe a sigh of relief. Because they'll never leave your side.*

_____

_____

_____

_____

_____

_____

# ANY EXCUSE TO HOARD MORE BOOKS!

Earlier in the book, we considered the idea of breaking away from the tyranny of keeping lists. If that didn't work for you, here is one last list to help you hang on to – and justify – your *tsundoku* lifestyle:

1. I reorganized my books alphabetically by author, but I didn't have any with a surname starting with 'X'.
2. How would you feel if you were the only full-price book in a bargain bin?
3. I wanted to go to Hawaii, but I didn't have enough money. So I bought a book about Hawaii instead.
4. You should've seen the look it was giving me . . .
5. You really ought to have at least one Icelandic author in your collection.
6. The author's pretty old, this might well be his last book.
7. This is the author's first published work: it's important to encourage her.
8. She's my favourite writer!
9. I haven't read anything by this author yet, and as I walked past it for the billionth time I felt judged.

10. I read something by this author once and thought it was dreadful. But everyone deserves a second chance.
11. This one came out on my birthday!
12. Money spent on books is always money well spent. I like to think of it as 'investing in my future'.
13. What if it goes out of print and I can never find it again?
14. It's signed by the author – how could I pass up an opportunity like that?
15. It was the only book I didn't have by this exuberant 17th-century poet.
16. Oh, this? I'm making a start on this tonight! Or tomorrow at the latest . . . or at worst, next weekend.
17. It was a first edition. How could I pass it up?
18. It was a second edition. How could I pass it up?
19. It was a third edition. How could I pass it up? (and so on . . .)
20. The colour of the cover matches my walls exactly!
21. Seeing my wishlist so full was making me antsy, so I had to empty it.
22. It costs less than going out for dinner and it's just as enjoyable!
23. I'm buying this to support my local bookshop and keep its doors open. Just doing my civic duty, no need to thank me.
24. It's from a publisher I wasn't familiar with.
25. It's from a publisher that never lets me down.
26. Everyone's read it except me!
27. What a coincidence: the title of this book is my mantra! I absolutely had to put it in plain sight, right at the top of that pile.
28. I need it for work.
29. I've bought it in the original language: it's good practice.
30. It's a cheap edition, it was a steal!
31. Well, I don't have any other vices . . .
32. It's a timeless classic.

ANY EXCUSE TO HOARD MORE BOOKS!

33. I've had a tough day, I deserve a little treat.
34. I've had a great day, I deserve to celebrate.
35. If I don't end up reading it, I can always give it to someone as a gift. Christmas is just around the corner.
36. You try keeping your hands off the graphic-novel section.
37. Yesterday? I don't remember buying any books yesterday. Can you imagine . . . ?
38. It's for that nine-hour flight I'm bound to take sooner or later.
39. I saw the three-for-two deal and turned it into an even better one: six-for-four! I'm a maths whiz!
40. You can blame it all on those damned BookTokers and their enticing reviews!
41. Recipe books don't count, everyone knows that.
42. I just happened to find some money in my pocket as I was walking past the bookshop. It was a sign.
43. It costs less than a pair of shoes and can take you much, much further away.
44. Don't worry, it all adds up perfectly: a book a day for a two-week holiday is a total of exactly 14 books. Not one more, not one less.
45. Go to a book launch without buying the book? No, my mother raised me better than that.
46. When the clocks change I'll have an extra hour of daylight to read.
47. I'm saving this trilogy in five parts for when I retire.
48. I saw the film, so it seemed a shame not to have solid proof that the book was better.
49. I just managed to clear that shelf . . . in the bathroom.
50. Sometimes you don't even have to read it: just take a big whiff of it and enjoy the dopamine rush.
51. One of my plants died and seeing all that empty space on the unit by the front door was making me sad.

52. My cousin's a structural engineer and he told me this was actually a load-bearing bookcase.
53. It just came out and it's all anyone's talking about. My social life is on the line here!
54. I walked past a bookshop and heard it calling out to me from the window display.
55. It was the last copy, just sitting there waiting for me.
56. Running my hands over that binding works better than taking my anxiety meds.
57. I was dressed exactly like the girl on the cover!
58. It costs less than a night in a hotel and it lasts longer.
59. The towers of books all over the living room make me feel safe, like I'm in a castle.
60. If there are no books on my bedside table, I feel lonely when I wake up in the middle of the night.
61. This one was on my list of New Year's resolutions. This way I can say I've completed at least one of them.
62. Don't you find there's something reassuring about the words 'complete and unabridged'?
63. When I retire, I'll have more time to read but less money to buy new books.
64. Any collection worth a damn contains at least ten books about cats.
65. What could I do? It was on the list of recommended books at the end of another book.
66. Actually, I'm reading more than one at a time.
67. I like lending them out to people. If they never get returned, I just buy a new copy.
68. All right, but this one doesn't count: who are you to question love at first sight?
69. It costs less than a relaxing massage and has the same effect.
70. I gave up on that thousand-page brick I started. Then I saw these three novels and realized they take up the same

ANY EXCUSE TO HOARD MORE BOOKS!

amount of space on the shelf, so I got them as a replacement.
71. I bought a book the moment I got to the station, because there's no better way to spend a train journey. Funny, I must have had the same thought last night when I put one in my bag.
72. But look, you can even colour this one in!
73. Oh, this pile? These are for my ongoing professional training...
74. I pressed a button by mistake and accidentally ordered my entire wishlist. Thirty books.
75. These? These are vintage, darling!
76. She's an up-and-coming young author. One day she'll be famous and I can say that I bought a first edition of her debut novel.
77. What if we get hit with a new lockdown and nobody can order anything online and I'm stuck with nothing to read?
78. I rearranged my books in colour order, but I didn't have a turquoise one for the transition from green to blue.
79. This one had a note above it saying 'recommended by Naomi'. I didn't want to disappoint her.
80. It's about to go out of print. It'll be worth a fortune in a few years.
81. I needed a new bag, so I bought five books and they gave me one for free...
82. I've started working out, but I find dumbbells so boring.
83. Oops, it fell on the floor! Suppose I'll have to buy it now...
84. I went out for a walk and found loads of four-leaf clovers. I needed somewhere to put them to dry ASAP.
85. It's hardly my fault if the author decided to write a 12-volume saga.
86. Someone left it at the till and I felt bad leaving it there all alone.

積ん読 – TSUNDOKU

87. It was in the wrong section. I just went to put it back, I swear. I haven't a clue how it ended up in my bag.
88. There are no limits on poetry books, right?
89. You recommended this one!
90. I didn't have my glasses on, but I could read the title from a distance. It seemed like a good idea to buy it so I could test my eyesight regularly.
91. In my entire collection, I didn't have a single book with exactly a thousand pages. I had to do something about it.
92. I wanted to check whether you could fit a book in my new, deceptively large handbag. Turns out you can get two in there!
93. Ugh, that stain on the coffee table just won't shift. I needed something to cover it up.
94. They chose it as the book of the month in that book club I gave up on. But by that point it was already on the list – and you don't take books off the list!
95. Yeah, but the author is the cousin of the guy I sat next to at school.
96. It's from a brand new bookshop that's just opened: what was I supposed to do, go in and then come out empty-handed?
97. The size and shape are perfect. My cat will love loafing on it.
98. If it's less than a hundred pages long then it counts as a little treat.
99. This one smelt even better than the others.
100. I didn't think I needed an excuse to buy a book!

# THE *TSUNDOKU* DIARY OF UNREAD BOOKS

What could be better than a diary to help us keep track of our reading? Notebooks, planners and apps can be useful, sure... but what about all those books we bought so enthusiastically but haven't quite managed to read yet (and probably never will)?

Never fear: *The* Tsundoku *Diary of Unread Books* is here! After all, why should *tsundoku*-ers have to lose out on the pleasure of writing down their thoughts on a book simply because they haven't read it? Trifles, details, technicalities...!

At this point, we are well aware that the volumes that fill our bookcases and our lives have been thoroughly stared at, leafed through, perhaps even cracked open and read (only a single random page, though) – and, above all, imagined. So it stands to reason that we've formed a solid idea of them.

This is a safe space where it doesn't matter if that idea isn't a perfect match for what is actually inside the book, or whether it's fiction or non-fiction, each of which has its own dedicated section below. This is the space for an unabashed outpouring of all the knowledge we have gleaned over our years of experience as readers.

積ん読 – TSUNDOKU

The space that allows our books to become the ideal version of themselves, exactly as we would like them to be.

The space that reminds us once again that, if we want them to change our lives for the better, they need only be close at hand.

THE *TSUNDOKU* DIARY OF UNREAD BOOKS

## ALL THE BOOKS I HAVEN'T READ – FICTION

Title:
Author:

✿ What inspired me to buy it?

✿ How I imagine the plot:

✿ The perfect ending to this book would be:

✿ This scene – if it had happened exactly like this – would have moved me to tears:

✿ The most loathsome character, even if only in my head:

✿ The atmospheres and landscapes that spring to mind the moment I look at the cover:

✿ The first sentence that grabbed my attention when I opened it to a random page:

I would recommend it to:

And when I have to explain why, I'll say:

積ん読 – TSUNDOKU

## ALL THE BOOKS I HAVEN'T READ – FICTION

Title:
Author:

- What inspired me to buy it?

- How I imagine the plot:

- The perfect ending to this book would be:

- This scene – if it had happened exactly like this – would have moved me to tears:

- The most loathsome character, even if only in my head:

- The atmospheres and landscapes that spring to mind the moment I look at the cover:

- The first sentence that grabbed my attention when I opened it to a random page:

I would recommend it to:

And when I have to explain why, I'll say:

THE *TSUNDOKU* DIARY OF UNREAD BOOKS

## ALL THE BOOKS I HAVEN'T READ – FICTION

Title:
Author:

- What inspired me to buy it?

- How I imagine the plot:

- The perfect ending to this book would be:

- This scene – if it had happened exactly like this – would have moved me to tears:

- The most loathsome character, even if only in my head:

- The atmospheres and landscapes that spring to mind the moment I look at the cover:

- The first sentence that grabbed my attention when I opened it to a random page:

I would recommend it to:

And when I have to explain why, I'll say:

積ん読 – TSUNDOKU

## ALL THE BOOKS I HAVEN'T READ – FICTION

Title:
Author:

✿ What inspired me to buy it?

✿ How I imagine the plot:

✿ The perfect ending to this book would be:

✿ This scene – if it had happened exactly like this – would have moved me to tears:

✿ The most loathsome character, even if only in my head:

✿ The atmospheres and landscapes that spring to mind the moment I look at the cover:

✿ The first sentence that grabbed my attention when I opened it to a random page:

I would recommend it to:

And when I have to explain why, I'll say:

THE *TSUNDOKU* DIARY OF UNREAD BOOKS

## ALL THE BOOKS I HAVEN'T READ – FICTION

Title:
Author:

✿ What inspired me to buy it?

✿ How I imagine the plot:

✿ The perfect ending to this book would be:

✿ This scene – if it had happened exactly like this – would have moved me to tears:

✿ The most loathsome character, even if only in my head:

✿ The atmospheres and landscapes that spring to mind the moment I look at the cover:

✿ The first sentence that grabbed my attention when I opened it to a random page:

I would recommend it to:

And when I have to explain why, I'll say:

積ん読 – TSUNDOKU

## ALL THE BOOKS I HAVEN'T READ – FICTION

Title:
Author:

✿ What inspired me to buy it?

✿ How I imagine the plot:

✿ The perfect ending to this book would be:

✿ This scene – if it had happened exactly like this – would have moved me to tears:

✿ The most loathsome character, even if only in my head:

✿ The atmospheres and landscapes that spring to mind the moment I look at the cover:

✿ The first sentence that grabbed my attention when I opened it to a random page:

I would recommend it to:

And when I have to explain why, I'll say:

THE *TSUNDOKU* DIARY OF UNREAD BOOKS

## ALL THE BOOKS I HAVEN'T READ – FICTION

Title:
Author:

✿ What inspired me to buy it?

✿ How I imagine the plot:

✿ The perfect ending to this book would be:

✿ This scene – if it had happened exactly like this – would have moved me to tears:

✿ The most loathsome character, even if only in my head:

✿ The atmospheres and landscapes that spring to mind the moment I look at the cover:

✿ The first sentence that grabbed my attention when I opened it to a random page:

I would recommend it to:

And when I have to explain why, I'll say:

積ん読 – TSUNDOKU

## ALL THE BOOKS I HAVEN'T READ – NON-FICTION

Title:
Author:

✿ What inspired me to buy it?

✿ I think that the key idea of it is:

✿ It really reminds me of this other book:

✿ What struck me the most about the cover is:

✿ Thanks to this book, I discovered that:

✿ The first sentence that grabbed my attention when I opened it to a random page:

✿ Leafing through this book made me want to find out more about:

I would recommend it to:

And when I have to explain why, I'll say:

THE *TSUNDOKU* DIARY OF UNREAD BOOKS

## ALL THE BOOKS I HAVEN'T READ – NON-FICTION

Title:
Author:

✿ What inspired me to buy it?

✿ I think that the key idea of it is:

✿ It really reminds me of this other book:

✿ What struck me the most about the cover is:

✿ Thanks to this book, I discovered that:

✿ The first sentence that grabbed my attention when I opened it to a random page:

✿ Leafing through this book made me want to find out more about:

I would recommend it to:

And when I have to explain why, I'll say:

積ん読 – TSUNDOKU

## ALL THE BOOKS I HAVEN'T READ – NON-FICTION

Title:
Author:

- What inspired me to buy it?

- I think that the key idea of it is:

- It really reminds me of this other book:

- What struck me the most about the cover is:

- Thanks to this book, I discovered that:

- The first sentence that grabbed my attention when I opened it to a random page:

- Leafing through this book made me want to find out more about:

I would recommend it to:

And when I have to explain why, I'll say:

THE *TSUNDOKU* DIARY OF UNREAD BOOKS

## ALL THE BOOKS I HAVEN'T READ – NON-FICTION

Title:
Author:

✿ What inspired me to buy it?

✿ I think that the key idea of it is:

✿ It really reminds me of this other book:

✿ What struck me the most about the cover is:

✿ Thanks to this book, I discovered that:

✿ The first sentence that grabbed my attention when I opened it to a random page:

✿ Leafing through this book made me want to find out more about:

I would recommend it to:

And when I have to explain why, I'll say:

積ん読 – TSUNDOKU

## ALL THE BOOKS I HAVEN'T READ – NON-FICTION

Title:
Author:

✿ What inspired me to buy it?

✿ I think that the key idea of it is:

✿ It really reminds me of this other book:

✿ What struck me the most about the cover is:

✿ Thanks to this book, I discovered that:

✿ The first sentence that grabbed my attention when I opened it to a random page:

✿ Leafing through this book made me want to find out more about:

I would recommend it to:

And when I have to explain why, I'll say:

THE *TSUNDOKU* DIARY OF UNREAD BOOKS

## ALL THE BOOKS I HAVEN'T READ – NON-FICTION

Title:
Author:

✿ What inspired me to buy it?

✿ I think that the key idea of it is:

✿ It really reminds me of this other book:

✿ What struck me the most about the cover is:

✿ Thanks to this book, I discovered that:

✿ The first sentence that grabbed my attention when I opened it to a random page:

✿ Leafing through this book made me want to find out more about:

I would recommend it to:

And when I have to explain why, I'll say: